LANCASHIRE COUNTY CRICKET CLUB: An A-Z

Dean Hayes

Copyright © Dean P. Hayes, 1997

Published by Sigma Leisure – an imprint of
Sigma Press, 1 South Oak Lane, Wilmslow, Cheshire SK9 6AR, England.

British Library Cataloguing in Publication Data
A CIP record for this book is available from the British Library.

ISBN: 1-85058-597-0

Typesetting and Design by: Sigma Press, Wilmslow, Cheshire.

Printed by: MFP Design & Print

Cover Design: The Agency, Wilmslow

Photographs: kindly supplied by Lancashire County Cricket Club, Lancashire Evening Post and Peter Stafford

Acknowledgments: The author wishes to thank the following in producing this book: Don Ambrose, Rev Malcolm Lorimer, Louise Turner and, finally, Graham Beech of Sigma Press for his support in producing books in this A-Z series.

ABRAHAMS, JOHN

John and his brothers came to England in the early 1960s when their father, Cec, a fine cricketer himself, joined Milnrow in the Central Lancashire League. It was only a few years later that the two of them were facing each other when Cec was professional with Rochdale and young John was playing for Milnrow.

His Lancashire debut came towards the end of the 1973 season and though it was another four years before he scored his maiden first-class century, he was one of the best fielders on the county circuit. It was 1982 before he was awarded his county cap, a summer in which he passed 1,000 runs for the first time. The following season he

John Abrahams leads out Lancashire with Mike Watkinson and Steve O'Shaughnessy not far behind.

replaced Clive Lloyd as captain on a number of occasions and so in 1984 when Lloyd was unavailable all season, he was the logical choice to replace him.

He was able to write himself into the county's record books in his first season in charge as Lancashire beat Warwickshire in the Benson and Hedges Cup Final at Lord's. Though he failed to score, Peter May made him the Man of the Match for 'his overall control and the glowing quality of his leadership'. That summer, Abrahams also made the highest score of his career, 201 not out against Warwickshire at Nuneaton.

He captained the county in 1985 but the following season, the Lancashire committee decided to turn back to Clive Lloyd. Abrahams responded with 1,134 runs in the Championship at 37.80, but after a well deserved Testimonial in 1988 he parted company with the county and went to play as professional for Heywood as well as representing Shropshire in 1989 and 1990.

AIGBURTH

Lancashire started to play first-class matches on the ground, from its first year, beginning with a game against Cambridge University in June 1881. It is said that because the wicket was not yet up to standard, Lancashire lost their only game of the summer!

Since then, first-class and limited-overs matches have been staged regularly. It is the oldest home venue outside Old Trafford and during the county's long association with Liverpool CC there have been many memorable performances on the ground.

In 1903, J.T. Tyldesley scored 248 and twenty-nine years later, Gloucestershire's Wally Hammond scored 264, still the highest score on the Aigburth ground.

Lancashire's Harry Dean took nine for 35 against Warwickshire at Aigburth and four years later in 1913, had match figures of seventeen for 91 against Yorkshire.

Gordon Greenidge took a particular liking to the ground, scoring 104 and 100 not out in a Championship game in 1983 and the following year scored 186 not out for the West Indies in a limited-overs match.

ALLOTT, PAUL

A former pupil of Altrincham Grammar School, he moved into the England Schools Cricket Association Under-19 side, bowling big 'in-swingers'. In 1976, he toured the Caribbean with the young side that included players of the calibre of David Gower and Mike Gatting and on his return, represented Cheshire in the Minor Counties League.

Allott attended Durham University and with future Lancashire players Graeme Fowler and Gehan Mendis in the side, it is little wonder that they won the UAU Championships. He made his Lancashire debut in 1978 and three years later produced the best figures of his career, taking eight for 48 against Northamptonshire. That season, he took 75 wickets for Lancashire and was awarded his county cap. He also turned in some other useful performances, taking six for 105 against Yorkshire and five for 94 against Surrey and these along with his figures in the Northamptonshire match led to him being selected

Paul Allott

for England in the Old Trafford Test against Australia. Here the Lancashire pace-bowler excelled with the bat, scoring an unbeaten 52.

Allott played for England in 13 Tests and in 1982 shared with Bob Willis in a record England tenth wicket stand of 70 against India at Lord's, whilst his best bowling figures at international level were six for 61 against the West Indies at Headingley in 1984.

He won a number of Man of the Match awards and also hit a six to clinch the Sunday League title in 1989. Yet for all his match-winning performances for the county, he failed to score a century, his highest score being 88 against Hampshire at Southampton in 1987.

He played the last of his games for the county in 1991, taking 549 first-class wickets at 24.46 runs apiece, a figure he would easily have exceeded had injuries not played such a decisive part in his career.

ALL TEN WICKETS

Three players have performed the feat of capturing all ten wickets in an innings for Lancashire. They are:

W. Hickton	10-46	v Hampshire at Old Trafford in 1870
J. Briggs	10-55	v Worcestershire at Old Trafford in 1900
R. Berry	10-102	v Worcestershire at Blackpool in 1953

APPEARANCES

The players with the highest number of appearances for Lancashire in the County Championship are as follows:

1.	Ernest Tyldesley	1909-1936	573
2.	Jack Sharp	1899-1925	518
3.	Johnny Tyldesley	1895-1923	507
4.	Cyril Washbrook	1933-1959	500
5.	Harry Makepeace	1906-1930	487
6.	Jack Iddon	1924-1945	483
7.	Frank Watson	1920-1937	456
8.	Ken Grieves	1949-1964	452
9.	David Hughes	1967-1991	436
10.	Brian Statham	1950-1968	430

David Hughes also leads the way in the Sunday League with 303 appearances and in the Gillette Cup/Nat West Trophy with 61 appearances. Jack Simmons has made the most appearances in the Benson and Hedges Cup competition with 83.

APPLEBY, ARTHUR

He played his early cricket with Enfield, where it was quickly discovered that he was a good fast bowler. He made his Lancashire debut against Surrey at Aigburth in 1866, taking six for 30. In fact, the Surrey secretary was so impressed, that he asked the young Appleby to play for the Gentlemen against the Players the following season.

Though his career for the county stretched over 22 seasons, due to business commitments, he only played in fifty-eight games. He took 245 wickets at 14.17 runs each with a best performance of nine for 25 against Sussex at Hove in 1877. A more than useful batsman, his best innings came in the Roses match at Bramall Lane in 1871 when he scored 99.

He turned down the chance of touring Australia twice, first with W.G. Grace in 1873, then with Lord Harris five years later, because of his corn-milling business. If he had gone with Lord Harris, there is little doubt that he would have joined Hornby, Royle and Schultz as Lancashire's first Test cricketers in the only Test played at Melbourne.

As a bowler, he took a deliberate and long run, bowling a fast round left arm, straight and with a good length and was still playing for Enfield in the summer before his death at the age of 59 in 1902.

ATHERTON, MICHAEL

Educated at Manchester Grammar School and Cambridge University, Mike Atherton made his Test debut at 21 and is currently captain of England. At Manchester Grammar School, he broke a number of batting records and was captain of the first XI at 15. The following year he captained the England Under-19 side and after making 73 as a freshman for Cambridge University against Essex, his choice of career was confirmed. Atherton captained both Cambridge and the Combined Universities in their enterprising giant-killing run of 1989, hitting three centuries, with a best of 151 not out against Middlesex.

Michael Atherton

He made his Lancashire debut against Warwickshire in 1987 and in scoring 1,193 first-class runs became the first batsman since Sussex's Paul Parker to make over 1,000 runs in a debut season.

In 1988, he scored his maiden first-class century for Lancashire against Sussex at Hove and the following summer was awarded his county cap. That season also saw him chosen to play for England in two Tests against Australia and in 1990 he became the youngest Englishman to score a Test hundred since David Gower in 1978.

In 1990, Atherton and Fairbrother added 364 for Lancashire's third wicket in the match against Surrey at The Oval, a county record and Atherton, who was a wily leg-spinner in his early days with the county , took six for 78 against Nottinghamshire at Trent Bridge.

His highest score for the county is 199 made against Durham at Gateshead Fell in 1992, a summer in which he scored 1,453 runs at 55.88. Atherton has also made centuries in each of the limited-overs competitions and for his country in a one-day international. He has played in 62 Tests with his highest score being 185 not out against South Africa in Johannesburg in November 1995.

ATTENDANCES

The highest attendance at Old Trafford on any one day is 46,000 (38,906 paid) to see the Lancashire v Yorkshire game in 1926. The gate of 78,617 for the whole match is the largest for a County Championship fixture. When England played Australia at Old Trafford in 1961, 120,417 saw the five-day match.

AUSTRALIA

In the 1878 match against the tourists, Barlow was nearly run out off the first ball of the match against Fred Spofforth, the Demon bowler, Hornby was leg-before to the second and Lancashire lost their first six wickets for 16 runs. The Red-Rose county were eventually all out for 97 (Spofforth nine for 53). Australia ended the day on 100 for one. However, the next day they lost their last nine wickets for 30 runs and so only led by 43. Their collapse just might have had something to do with the tourists' attendance at the Queen's Hotel the night before when a banquet was held in their honour. The third day was interrupted by rain and the tourists were 73 short of victory with all their wickets intact when the game was abandoned.

Ten years later, Lancashire inflicted the Australians first defeat of the summer, it was also the Red-Rose county's first victory over them in five meetings. Lancashire won by 23 runs with Napier having match figures of seven for 102 and hitting a quick-fire 37 in Lancashire's second innings.

In 1912, Lancashire beat the Australians twice, though due to the Club sticking an extra sixpence on the price of admission, the crowds were poor.

When the Australians visited Old Trafford in 1938, Eddie Phillipson had the great satisfaction of dismissing Don Bradman for 12, though in the second innings, Bradman scored a century in 73 minutes!

In 1948, Cyril Washbrook was given the Australian match as his benefit. Don Bradman captained Australia but did not enforce the follow-on and scored an unbeaten 133 on what was his last appearance at the ground. Lancashire were able to play out time, although with five minutes remaining, Bradman took the new ball and Ray Lindwall bowled Ikin and Pollard with successive deliveries!

In 1961, Lancashire recorded their highest score against the Australians with Geoff Pullar scoring almost half his side's total of 346. Lancashire's record of first-class matches v Australia is:

P.	W.	L.	D.	Tied
43	5	17	21	–

BAILS

When Lancashire's William Huddleston was bowled by Burrows of Worcestershire at Old Trafford on 29 June 1911, the bail travelled from the stumps, 67 yards 6 inches – the longest recorded distance!

In 1897, Lancashire's Arthur Mold bowled Surrey's George Lohmann and sent a bail 63 yards 6 inches.

BARBER, BOB

He made his debut for Lancashire in 1954 when still only 18 and was midway between Ruthin College and Cambridge University.

In 1960, he became the second Light Blue captain of Lancashire, getting off to a flying start with two victories over Yorkshire, the first time since 1893 that the Red-Rose county had done the double over their rivals.

Bob Barber was a superb all-round cricketer. An attacking left-handed batsman, a right arm leg-break bowler and an excellent close to the wicket fielder. He also captained the side in 1961 and then played one more season under Joe Blackledge before leaving to join Warwickshire.

He had played in 155 matches in his nine seasons at Old Trafford, scoring 6,760 runs at an average of 28.28 and taking 152 wickets at 31.36 runs each.

At Edgbaston, caution gave way to attack and he became one of the most attractive batsmen in the country. He played 28 times for England with a top score of 185 at Sydney, one of the greatest innings in Ashes history. An adventurous cricketer, Bob Barber was seen by many as an individualist with a mind and temperament all of his own.

BARDSWELL, GERALD

After captaining Uppingham, Gerald Bardswell obtained a Blue at Oxford University, joining Lancashire in 1894. He also captained the University in 1897.

Bardswell was the first bowler of real quality to captain the county after bursting on the scene in Lancashire's victory over Middlesex at Lord's in 1894. He was officially appointed captain of Lancashire in 1899 but unfortunately due to business commitments he only led the side in four matches and the captaincy returned to Archie MacLaren. He toured North America with Lord Harris in 1894-95 and West Indies in 1896-97 before playing the last of his 21 games for Lancashire in 1902. He died tragically in 1908 at the age of only 33 after he had seemingly recovered from an operation in New Orleans.

BARLOW, RICHARD

As a boy, Richard Barlow had batted and bowled left-handed but on the advice of his father, he started to bat right-handed and though over the years he acquired the reputation of a stone-waller, it is interesting to note that Barlow's contemporaries never referred to him as a slow player.

On numerous occasions, Barlow saved Lancashire from defeat by his resolute defence. He carried his bat through an innings on twelve occasions and many times was the last wicket to fall. In 1884 while playing for the North of England against Australia, he scored 10 not out in the North's first innings total of 91. The Australians were bowled out for 100 and then Barlow and Flowers added 158 for the sixth wicket with Barlow being the last man out for a superb 101. He completed a remarkable all-round performance by returning match figures of ten for 45.

In 1882 when Lancashire were bowled out for 69 in the match against Nottinghamshire at Trent Bridge, Barlow carried his bat for two and a half hours, scoring just five runs!

As a bowler, Barlow was closer to medium-pace than slow, accurate and could spin the ball away from the bat. He took 736 wickets for the county at 13.60 runs apiece.

He played in 17 Test matches, scoring 591 runs and taking 35 wickets and to this day, is the only cricketer to be selected for England with the specific intention that he should open both the batting and the bowling. He played his last game for Lancashire in 1891 after being left out of a number of end of season fixtures and having a disagreement with the committee.

Richard Barlow designed his own headstone for his grave in Layton Cemetery, Blackpool. It shows a set of stumps with the ball passing through middle and leg and at the bottom the words 'Bowled at last!'

BARNES, SYDNEY

Sydney Barnes was a professional cricketer for more than 45 years and in all forms of cricket, took 6,225 wickets at 8.31 runs each. Twelve times in his career he took all ten wickets in an innings. In 1906 while playing for Porthill against Leek Highfield, he scored 76 with the bat, then took ten for 12 with the ball. A year later he took 112 wickets at 3.91 runs each, captured all ten Leek Highfield wickets again and did the hat-trick twice in one innings against Silverdale.

After playing five matches for Warwickshire between 1893 and 1896, the Smethwick-born bowler joined Rishton in the Lancashire League, doubling as a groundsman.

He played two seasons for Lancashire and in 1902 was the county's leading wicket-taker with 84 wickets. However, his best season for the Red-Rose county came in 1903 when he took 131 wickets at 17.85 runs each. Those were his only full seasons in first-class cricket and having played in only 46 matches for Lancashire, Barnes left county cricket.

He played in 27 Tests for England, taking a remarkable 189 wickets at 16.43 runs each and in just even Tests against South Africa he took 83 wickets. He was a remarkable man and at the age of 55 he headed the English first-class averages and at 56 bowled unchanged for three hours and took eight for 41 bowling for the Minor Counties against South Africa. At the age of 67, he was still taking wickets as a club professional.

He died in 1967 at the age of 94, modestly admitting that had he been playing cricket in the modern era, he could quite easily have taken 500 Test wickets.

BENEFITS

Lancashire's first beneficiary was Fred Reynolds in 1870. In 1894, Lord Hawke, the Yorkshire captain refused to play on a wicket which had been covered and caused Johnny Briggs' Benefit match to be over in two days. In 1897, Frank Sugg had a Benefit when 24,000 people came on the first day but play was not possible on the other days due to torrential rain. The following year, George Baker's Benefit was affected because Lancashire lost by ten wickets on the second day.

In 1900, fast bowler Arthur Mold was unwell and so had to sit out his Benefit match, whilst three years later, two Yorkshiremen, Willis Cuttell and Charlie Smith had Benefits for Lancashire in the same season.

¤   In 1934 during George Duckworth's Benefit match against Surrey, Jack Hobbs scored his last first-class century.

¤   In 1967, Geoff Pullar chose the Roses match against Yorkshire
    at Old Trafford for his Benefit match, but not a ball was
    bowled!

¤   In 1995, Neil Fairbrother earned £206,000 for his Benefit, the
    largest amount by a Lancashire player.

¤   Five Lancashire players have had both a Benefit and a Testimo-
    nial for the county. They are Ernest Tyldesley, Cyril Wash-
    brook, Brian Statham, Clive Lloyd and David Hughes.

BENSON AND HEDGES CUP

This, the third of the regular limited-overs competitions in Britain,
was started in 1972, contested by the then 17 first-class counties,
Minor Counties(North) and (South) and Cambridge University. Oxford and Cambridge alternated each season until 1975 when they
formed a Combined Universities team. Scotland entered in 1980
when the Minor Counties were restricted to one team. Four regional
leagues determine two teams from each to go through to quarter-finals
of a knock-out competition. Matches are played over 55 overs with
bowlers restricted to 11 overs each.

The first matches were commenced on 29 April 1972, but none was
completed that day. They were extended over the next three days.
The first winners of the trophy were Leicestershire who defeated
Yorkshire in the final.

Lancashire have won the trophy on four occasions with the following results in the finals:

1984	Warwickshire 139, Lancashire 140 for four
1990	Lancashire 241, Worcestershire 172
1995	Lancashire 274 for seven, Kent 239
1996	Northamptonshire 223, Lancashire 224 for nine

The county also reached the final in 1991 and 1993 and were
semi-finalists in 1973, 1974, 1982 and 1983.

When Lancashire won the trophy in 1984, an uneventful final was
highlighted only by Adjudicator Peter May's choice of John Abrahams as Man of the Match. He had been dismissed for 0 but won the
award for his leadership qualities.

On their way to the 1990 final, the match with Hampshire at Old Trafford was called off twice due to bad weather but in the first meeting, Lancashire broke all records with 352 for six, featuring a third wicket partnership of 244 between Atherton and Fairbrother. Sadly, due to the bad weather this record will not stand.

Lancashire's full record in the Benson and Hedges Cup is as follows:

P.	W.	L.	No Result	
128	82	39	7	(of these one match was abandoned without a ball being bowled)

Other Benson and Hedges Cup records include:

Highest Innings Total	353 for seven v Nottinghamshire at Old Trafford in 1995.
Lowest Completed Innings Total	82 v Yorkshire at Bradford in 1972.
Highest Individual Innings	136 by G. Fowler v Sussex at Old Trafford in 1991.
Best Bowling Performance	6 for 10 by C. Croft v Scotland at Old Trafford in 1982.
Highest Partnership	250 for 2nd wicket by J. Gallian and J. Crawley v Warwickshire at Edgbaston in 1995
Most Gold Awards	10 by B. Wood.

BERRY, BOB

The first cricketer to be capped by three counties, Bob Berry started his career with Denton St Lawrence before moving on to Longsight. He made his Lancashire debut in 1948 and two years later was awarded his county cap. His two Test appearances also came in the summer of 1950 and in the first at Old Trafford, he returned match figures of nine for 116. He toured Australia with Freddie Brown's 1950-51 team but not being the greatest spinner of the ball, he did not play in any of the Tests.

In July 1953, Bob Berry took all ten Worcestershire wickets for 102 runs in the match at Blackpool. After another season with Lancashire and a total of 259 first-class wickets he left to join Worcestershire. He took five for 65 on his debut against the South Africans and went on to take 250 wickets for them, before ending his first-class career with Derbyshire, for whom he took 97 wickets. In a county career that

finished in 1962, Bob Berry took 703 first-class wickets with a best
for Lancashire of ninety-eight wickets at 18.97 runs each in 1953.

BLACKLEDGE, JOE

Appointed Lancashire captain in 1962, Joe Blackledge played his
cricket for Chorley in the Northern League and had no first-class
experience whatsoever. It was a disastrous season for Lancashire as
they finished second from bottom, their lowest-ever position in the
County Championship. The county won only two matches all summer, but they were against counties who were top of the table at the
time. At the end of the season, Blackledge returned to League cricket
and his business life. He currently serves the county as a Committee
member.

BLACKPOOL

Blackpool was granted its first inter-county match in 1906 when
Leicestershire provided the opposition and followed a first-class
three day game between An England XI and the visiting West Indian
tourists. The first was rain interrupted but in the second, Lancashire
defeated Leicestershire by an innings and 41 runs. Jack Sharp made
111, the first century on the ground and Bill Gregson took five for 8,
including a hat-trick.

Leicestershire and Warwickshire were beaten in 1907 and 1908 but
apart from a badly rain-affected game against Warwickshire in 1910,
rearranged at the last minute after the original match at Old Trafford
had been postponed because of the death of King Edward VII, there
was no further county cricket at Blackpool until 1923. Glamorgan
were Lancashire's next opponents on the ground and they were
heavily beaten with Cec Parkin returning match figures of fifteen for
95.

In 1925, the ground was renamed Stanley Park and prior to the
match against Essex, a new pavilion opened. In addition to the county
fixtures and the visiting tourists, the Blackpool Cricket Festival
featured such games as North v South, Gentlemen v Players and
Lancashire v various England XI's.

During the Second World War, the ground was commandeered by

the RAF for training and a large hangar was erected near the entrance for that purpose. County games recommenced in 1946 but it was eleven years later before Lancashire suffered their first defeat at the ground, at the hands of Northamptonshire.

In 1953, Bob Berry took all ten Worcestershire wickets as Lancashire won by 18 runs. In 1954, a new scorebox was built and the new County Stand completed in time for the visit of the 1957 West Indians and that first defeat by Northamptonshire. In 1959, Jim Stewart of Warwickshire hit the record number of sixes in a first-class match when he bludgeoned 17 off the Lancashire attack.

Lancashire began to lose a little more regularly at Stanley Park and in 1966 were bowled out for 62 by Kent with Derek Underwood taking six for 9. The following year, Hampshire were dismissed for just 39 with John Savage taking five for 1.

Perhaps one of the most dramatic matches at the ground came in 1977 when Middlesex's Edmonds (six for 27) and Emburey (six for 8) demolished Lancashire to give their side victory by 91 runs. They then had to wait for the other results to see if they had won the Championship. Eventually they heard the news that the results had gone against them and they had to share the Championship with Kent.

BOND, JACK

After leaving Bolton School, Jack Bond joined Walkden in the Bolton League, averaging 44 in his only full season before moving to Radcliffe, where he was given great encouragement and advice from professional Cec Pepper.

Making his Lancashire debut in 1955, he was dismissed for 0 and 1 by Lock and Laker in the match against Surrey. A few seasons later, he delighted in taking a century off both bowlers. He scored the first of his 14 centuries for Lancashire in 1959 when he made 101 not out against Nottinghamshire at Trent Bridge.

In 1961, he was awarded his county cap after scoring three centuries. The following summer was the best of his career, as he scored 2,125 runs and a career best 157 against Hampshire at Old Trafford.

Appointed captain of Lancashire in 1968, he led the county to the Sunday League title the following season, its first year of inception.

Jack Bond

In 1970, Lancashire finished third in the County Championship, retained the John Player Sunday League title and won the Gillette Cup for the first time. The 1971 season saw Lancashire maintain third position in the Championship but the John Player League title went to Worcestershire. However, after beating Gloucestershire in a dramatic semi-final, Bond led Lancashire to victory over Kent in the Gillette Cup Final . It was Bond's unbelievable catch to dismiss Asif that turned the game.

In 1972, Bond led Lancashire to their third successive Gillette Cup Final where they beat Warwickshire by four wickets. At the end of the season, he joined Lancashire's coaching staff but later left to captain Nottinghamshire.

He also returned to Old Trafford to become manager, helping Lancashire to win the Benson and Hedges Cup in 1984. A former first-class umpire and Test selector, he will always be remembered for his tremendous contribution to Lancashire cricket.

BOOKS

Among the many books that have been written about Lancashire County Cricket Club are:

Lancashire County Cricket by Rex Pogson, 1952

Old Trafford by John Marshall, 1972

A History of Lancashire County Cricket by John Kay, 1974

Lancashire Cricketers 1865-1988 by Rev Malcolm Lorimer

Lancashire Cricketing Greats by Dean Hayes, 1989

Red Roses Crest their Caps by Eric Midwinter, 1989

The History of Lancashire CCC by Peter Wynne Thomas, 1989

From the Stretford End by Brian Bearshaw, 1990

A Who's Who of Lancashire by Robert Brooke, 1990

Heads or Tails? Lancashire Captains 1865-1991 by Roy Cavanagh

BREARLEY, WALTER

After gaining a reputation as a fast bowler with Bolton and Manchester, he joined Lancashire and made his debut for the county in 1902.

Brearley came into his own in 1904 when Lancashire ran away with the County Championship and was considered the best amateur fast bowler in the country. He took 95 wickets that summer but would have had many more if he hadn't missed the whole of August through injury.

The 1905 season was without doubt Brearley's best, as he took 133 wickets at 19 runs apiece for Lancashire and 181 in all first-class matches. In the match against Somerset at Old Trafford he took nine for 47 before lunch on the first day and then accomplished the remarkable feat of four wickets in four balls as the visitors batted again. He went on to take eight for 90 in the second innings to finish with the match analysis of seventeen for 137. His form that summer led to him gaining Test recognition and he played in the last two Tests against Australia at Old Trafford and the Oval. Also that season, playing for Lancashire, England and the Gentlemen, he took the wicket of Victor Trumper on six occasions in nine innings.

Quite a volatile character, Brearley had numerous brushes with authority and on a couple of occasions submitted his resignation following differences of opinion with the Lancashire Committee. Happily for all concerned, the matters were settled amicably and he continued to play for Lancashire.

Brearley thrived on the big occasion and in fourteen Roses games he took 125 wickets at 16 runs each. With the bat, Brearley was an automatic Number 11 and on his way to the crease, would ignore the gate and leap the fence and almost run to the wicket! Brearley frequently scorned the use of gloves and only occasionally wore pads!

For the county in his short career, he took 690 wickets at 18.70 runs apiece in just 106 matches. There is no doubt that Old Trafford was always a livelier place for his presence and for the cricket he played there.

BRIGGS, JOHNNY

One of cricket's most gifted all-rounders, Johnny Briggs was born in Sutton-in-Ashfield in Nottinghamshire, but when he was 14, the year after his father had been appointed the first professional at Widnes Cricket Club, he moved, along with the rest of his family, from Sutton to make their home there.

Johnny Briggs played in the Lancashire Colts XI in May 1879 and later that month whilst still only 16, made his first-class debut against his native county Nottinghamshire, top-scoring with 36.

Over the years, his bowling improved as he reduced his pace to slow-medium and probably because the left-arm spinner was asked to do more than his share of bowling when Crossland was disqualified from playing for the county. In 1885, the year of Crossland's disqualification, Briggs headed the county bowling averages with 79 wickets at 10.50 runs apiece.

He had made the first of his 33 Test appearances at Adelaide during the 1884-85 tour of Australia, playing as a batsman, and scored 121 in his second Test at Melbourne. In 1886 he played in all three home Tests against Australia and though he wasn't required to bowl at Old Trafford, he had match figures of eleven for 74 at Lord's and took six for 58 and scored 53 at the Oval.

During the summer of 1888 he claimed twelve wickets for 94 runs in the Test series against the Australians and playing against the same opposition, took nine for 49 for Lancashire, thirteen for 40 for Lord Londesborough's XI and ten for 80 for Shaw and Shrewsbury's XI. That summer he topped the bowling averages with 160 wickets and scored over 800 runs. Wisden introduced its gallery of Six Great Bowlers for the first time and Johnny Briggs was one of the six selected.

Two days after his marriage to Alice Burgess, he was playing for Lancashire and made the highest score of his career, 186 against Surrey at Aigburth, sharing in a tenth wicket stand of 173 with Dick Pilling.

Touring South Africa with England in 1888-89 he created new Test records by his analysis of eight for 11 (all bowled) in the second innings of the Test at Cape Town and fifteen for 28 all in the same day's play. The fifteen wicket record still stands today as the most taken by one bowler in a day's Test cricket.

Johnnny Briggs

In 1891-92, he toured Australia and performed the hat-trick in the second Test at Sydney. He is still the only cricketer to have scored a hundred and performed the hat-trick in a Test match.

For Lancashire, Briggs took 1,696 wickets at 15.60 runs apiece and scored over 10,000 runs in his twenty seasons of first-class cricket. He is the only Lancashire player to have taken over 1,000 wickets and scored over 10,000 runs for the county and his total of wickets is only bettered by Brian Statham.

He relished Roses matches and took 170 wickets in these meetings at less than 16 runs each. His final season for the county was 1900 when he took 120 wickets at 17.40 runs each, including for the first time in his career, ten wickets for 55 runs against Worcestershire at Old Trafford.

He had been admitted to hospital in July 1899 and though he was not discharged until March of the following year, he seemed to have recovered. However, at the end of the season he fell ill again and readmitted to Cheadle Asylum, where he died on 11 January 1902.

BROTHERS

There have been 28 instances of brothers playing for Lancashire. Edmund Butler Rowley who captained Lancashire from 1866 to 1879 and in his last season, led the side to a share in the County Championship title came from a family of seven boys. One of his brothers, Alexander Butler was also a fine player and administrator and became Lancashire President between 1874 and 1880.

The four Steel brothers of whom Allan Gibson Steel was the most famous, considered second only to W.G. Grace as the country's finest all-rounder appeared together in one match. This was against Surrey at Aigburth in a match which Lancashire lost by 29 runs after needing 133 for victory. D.Q. Steel scored 0 and 13, H.B. 18 and 0, E.E. 22 and 7 and A.G. 39 and 20 as well as taking one wicket.

J.T. Tyldesley who played in 31 Tests and scored 31,949 runs for Lancashire at 41.38 was regarded as the greatest batsman the county have ever had until his younger brother Ernest came along to challenge him. Ernest scored 34,222 runs at 45.20 yet for those who saw both players, J.T. was regarded as the better player of the two.

Not related to the previous Tyldesleys were four brothers who also played for Lancashire. Billy, who was a left-handed batsman and killed in the last year of the First World War; James, who at one time looked liked developing into a useful fast bowler; Harry who played in a few matches and Richard, who was by far the most successful, taking 1,449 wickets for the county at 16.65 runs apiece.

One of four first-class cricketing brothers, Geoff Edrich reached 1,000 runs in a season on eight occasions and was signed with his brother Eric on their pre-war reputations. Eric only played until 1948 but did score 121 against Yorkshire at Headingley in the Roses match of that year.

CAMBRIDGE UNIVERSITY

Lancashire's only defeat in their Championship-winning season of 1881 came in the opening fixture of the summer against Cambridge University at Aigburth. G.B. Studd, who opened the innings for the University carried his bat for 106 and thus had the distinction of recording the first century on the ground in first-class cricket. Cambridge were 67 for five but thanks to Studd, recovered to score 187. A.G. Steel was in the University side, as was another Lancashire player in the Revd John Napier, who took six for 22 as the Red-Rose county were dismissed for 71. Following on, Lancashire were bowled out for 153 with Steel taking five for 69. Needing just 38 to win, the University lost four wickets in reaching their target with J.E.K. Studd out for a duck in the fifteenth maiden over the innings!

The two sides met again in 1907 after a gap of twenty-five years, with Lancashire losing by the unbelievable margin of an innings and 204 runs! Lancashire's record of first-class matches v Cambridge University is:

P.	W.	L.	D.	Tied
44	12	7	25	0

CAPTAINS

This is the complete list of Lancashire's captains:

E.B. Rowley	1866-79
A.N. Hornby	1880-91
S.M. Crosfield and A.N. Hornby	1892-93
A.C. MacLaren	1894-96
A.N. Hornby	1897-98
A.C. MacLaren and G.R. Bardswell	1899
A.C. MacLaren	1900-07
A.H. Hornby	1908-14
M.N. Kenyon	1919-22
J. Sharp	1923-25
L. Green	1926-28
P.T. Eckersley	1929-35
W.H.L. Lister	1936-39
J.A. Fallows	1946
K. Cranston	1947-48
N.D. Howard	1949-53
C. Washbrook	1954-59
R.W. Barber	1960-61
J.F. Blackledge	1962
K.J. Grieves	1963-64
J.B. Statham	1965-67
J.D. Bond	1968-72
D. Lloyd	1973-77
F.C. Hayes	1978-80
C.H. Lloyd	1981-83
J. Abrahams	1984-85
C.H. Lloyd	1986
D.P. Hughes	1987-91
N.H. Fairbrother	1992-93
M. Watkinson	1994-

CARRYING BAT

Jim Ricketts was the first Lancashire player to bat through an innings and he did this when he played his first match for the county from 30 May to 1 June 1867 against Surrey at the Oval. To score a century in those days was a notable feat, but to open and bat through the innings for 195 not out was nothing short of incredible.

Richard Barlow's reputation was as a stonewalling batsman and he claimed to have batted right through an innings fifty times, including an innings of five not out in two and a half hours against Nottinghamshire in 1882.

Albert Ward was an opening batsman with an ideal temperament and he batted through the innings five times for Lancashire. Harry Makepeace carried his bat through an innings for Lancashire on four occasions, whilst Charlie Hallows who opened the innings with Makepeace in his early years, achieved the feat on six occasions, including an innings of 152 not out against Yorkshire at Old Trafford in 1929.

Other Lancashire players who have carried their bat through an innings for the county are A.N. Hornby, Len Hopwood, Cyril Washbrook, Jack Ikin, Winston Place, Brian Booth and most recently, Gehan Mendis, who carried his bat for 65 not out against Glamorgan at Swansea in 1988.

CASTLETON

Castleton Cricket Club was formed in connection with the Rochdale Football Club in December 1869. After successfully hosting prestigious matches such as an England XI v XXII of Castleton and Lancashire v Yorkshire United, it was decided that Castleton should host only the second county match outside of Old Trafford since the formation of the County Club in 1864.

There was a good crowd drawn from the local mills and tanneries to see Lancashire play Kent on 15 June 1876. Kent fielded a strong side captained by Lord Harris and included five players who went on to represent England. Lancashire batted first and scored 181 thanks to 65 from A.N. Hornby. Kent were shot out for 56 with Bill McIntyre taking six for 30 and Alec Watson four for 26. Following-on, only Lord

Harris with 82 offered any resistance to Watson, who took seven for 61 and performed the hat-trick, the first by a Lancashire player.

Lancashire won by ten wickets on the second day, but with the early finish, Castleton lost money. The guarantors were forced to stand the loss, but the club were never again to be graced by the county in a first-class fixture.

CATCHES

The most catches in an innings by a Lancashire player is six, a feat achieved by Dick Tyldesley (v Hampshire at Aigburth 1921) and Ken Grieves (v Sussex at Old Trafford 1951). In this latter match, Grieves held eight catches in the match, the Lancashire record.

The Australian-born all-rounder also holds the county record for the most catches in a season, 63 in 1950 and for the most catches in a career, 555 – 206 more than second placed Archie MacLaren.

CENTURIES

The first century scored for the county was by Yorkshireman Roger Iddison, who made 106 against Surrey in 1866, whilst the first amateur to score a century for Lancashire was Rev Frank Wright, who made an unbeaten 120 against Sussex in 1869.

Four Lancashire players have scored a century on their first appearance for the county. They are Jim Ricketts, 195 not out v Surrey at the Oval in 1867; Archie MacLaren, 108 v Sussex at Brighton in 1890; Ralph Whitehead, 131 not out v Nottinghamshire at Old Trafford in 1908; and Gary Yates, 106 v Nottinghamshire at Trent Bridge in 1990.

In the match against Somerset in 1904, four Lancashire players scored centuries in one innings – Archie MacLaren 151, A.H. Hornby 114, Johnny Tyldesley 103 and Willis Cuttell 101.

Only Ernest Tyldesley and Jack Iddon have scored centuries against every first-class county, whilst Tyldesley is also the only Lancashire player to accomplish the feat of scoring four hundreds in successive innings, which he did in both 1926 and 1928.

When Graeme Fowler scored centuries in each innings of the match against Warwickshire at Southport in 1982, he had a runner because of injury!

In 1983, Lancashire's Steve O'Shaughnessy equalled the time for the fastest first-class hundred. In the game against Leicestershire at Old Trafford, he was fed full tosses and long hops by two non-bowlers in the hope of expediting a declaration! The following players have scored the most centuries for Lancashire:

1.	Ernest Tyldesley	90
2.	Johnny Tyldesley	73
3.	Cyril Washbrook	58
4.	Charlie Hallows	52
5.	Frank Watson	49
6.	Jack Iddon	46
7.	Harry Makepeace	42
8.	David Lloyd	37
9.	Eddie Paynter	36
	Jack Sharp	36

CHAMPIONSHIPS

Champions	1881, 1897, 1904, 1926, 1927, 1928, 1930, 1934
Joint Champions	1879, 1882, 1889, 1950

In 1879, Lancashire shared the title with Nottinghamshire, as each side had lost only one match in county games. The one defeat that season which cost Lancashire their first outright Championship was inflicted by Yorkshire at Bramall Lane, where Willie Bates scored the first ever Roses century.

A.N. Hornby led Lancashire to the 1881 title in only his second season in charge. They won 10 of their 13 Championship matches and drew the other three, with Hornby being the first Lancastrian to pass 1,000 runs in a season.

Attempting to lead Lancashire to a second successive title, Hornby had to be content to share the title with Nottinghamshire again, as both sides lost only one game.

Because of a new points system, devised the previous year, Lancashire were accredited joint Champions with Nottinghamshire and Surrey. The highlights of the season being double victories over Surrey and Yorkshire.

In 1897, Lancashire won the title outright for a second time. They made a fine start to the season, with five early successes before losing to Surrey, who, in fact did the double over them. The title seemed to be heading to the Oval, but incredibly Surrey lost to lowly Somerset in their last match and the title returned to Old Trafford.

Under Archie MacLaren's captaincy, Lancashire won 16 and drew the rest of their 26 matches in 1904 to take the title outright for a third time.

Lancashire next won the title in 1926, by a narrow margin from Yorkshire. Though the Red-Rose county lost two matches and Yorkshire went through the summer unbeaten, Lancashire did win 17 matches, three more than their rivals.

The following season brought an even harder tussle for the title. Lancashire's slow batting almost cost them the Championship. The county's policy was to wear down the opposition bowling and then in the evening try to take toll of tired opposition. That it wasn't always carried out must be apportioned to the temperament of some of the team. However, though they only won 10 matches, they only lost once, to Sussex and ended the season two points ahead of Nottinghamshire.

Lancashire's third successive title, gained in 1928 saw them win 15 of their 28 fixtures and draw the rest. It was a vintage season for all the batsmen with Hallows scoring 1,000 runs in May. County captain Leonard Green retired at the end of the season after leading Lancashire to three titles in three years.

In 1930, Lancashire again went through the season undefeated and after a close struggle, regained the title, with captain Peter Eckersley's tactical awareness playing an important part. The county set out to avoid defeat in vital matches and then went all out for victory against the weaker opposition.

The summer of 1934 saw Lancashire win the title outright for the eighth and last time. Eckersley as captain won the toss more times than most and this resulted in Lancashire batting first and when in a strong position, declaring. Though the attack lacked a McDonald or a Parkin, it did contain bowling for almost every type of wicket.

In 1950, Lancashire ended the season as joint champions with Surrey, their last Championship to date. Going into their last match against Surrey at the Oval, Lancashire only needed four points from a first innings lead, assuming Surrey didn't win the match to take the title outright. The match ended in a boring draw but Surrey won their last match to share the Championship.

CHRISTMAS CARD

The feeling between Lancashire and Nottinghamshire was far from friendly and when Nottinghamshire refused to play the Red-Rose county because of the presence of Crossland and Nash in the team, two Nottinghamshire-born players, Lancashire sent a Christmas Card to Trent Bridge: It read: Cricketing Rules drawn up by the Notts CCC 1883-84.

Rule 1

That in playing Lancashire, the Lancashire men shall not be allowed to use bats, but only broom handles.

Rule 2

That Lancashire shall not be allowed any bowler and if so, no stumps to be used; and the Notts captain to select the bowler.

Rule 3

That both umpires shall be strictly Notts men.

Rule 4

That in case there is any fear that Notts should lose, even under these rules, the Notts men do leave the field and refuse to finish the game.

CLERGYMEN

The three clergymen to have played for Lancashire, are Rev Vernon Royle, Rev John Russell Napier and the Rev Frank Wright. The latter was chosen for the county's first game against Middlesex in 1865 but dropped out. However, in 1869 he scored 120 not out, the first-ever century by a Lancashire player in what was only his second match.

The Rev John Napier only played in two games for the county. In the first, he was instrumental in Lancashire beating the Australians for the first time in five encounters, having match figures of seven for 102 and top-scoring with a second innings score of 37. In his second appearance against Yorkshire at Bramall Lane, he took four wickets in fourteen balls without conceding a run – his last two wickets in two balls – yet he never bowled for Lancashire again!

The Rev Vernon Royle was one of the finest cover-point fielders in English cricket and it was often said that he was worth his place in a team for his fielding alone.

COOK, LOL

COUNTY CRICKETERS.

L. COOK,
LANCASHIRE.

A man of generous girth, Lol Cook was really two bowlers in one. On a fast wicket, he bowled at a brisk medium-pace, swinging the ball away from the bat and was able to send down a much faster delivery without any change in his action. If there was any rain in the air, Cook would bowl a slowish off-break from around the wicket. But whether he was bowling off-breaks or at a medium-pace, the Preston-born bowler sent down very few bad balls. His career figures for Lancashire of 821 wickets at 21.36 runs apiece, tell little of the immense amount of hard work Cook got through.

In 1920, he took 150 wickets, including seven for 8 in the match against Derbyshire at Chesterfield, as he turned in one of the finest pieces of controlled bowling seen in Lancashire cricket for a good number of years. The following season he was chosen for the Players v Gentlemen at Lord's after he had taken 91 wickets by the middle of July on hard pitches. He ended the season with 148 wickets at 22.90 runs each and in 1922, took 142 wickets to complete a hundred wickets in three successive seasons.

CRANSTON, KEN

Despite spending only two years in first-class cricket, Ken Cranston captained England, played in eight Tests and took four wickets in six balls against South Africa.

Cranston scored a century for Lancashire 2nd XI against Yorkshire and during the Second World War, played for the Royal Navy, Combined Services and Club Cricket Conference.

After the hostilities, Cranston began to make a name for himself with Neston in the Liverpool Competition. Despite embarking on a career in dentistry, the Aigburth-born all-rounder was asked to captain Lancashire and in 1947 he led them to third place in the County Championship. After just 13 first-class matches for the Red-Rose county, he was chosen for England. In eight Tests, he scored 209 runs and captured 18 wickets.

In both his seasons with Lancashire he came very near to doing the 'double' of 1,000 runs and 100 wickets. Yet at the end of the 1948 season, he decided to return to dentistry, happy to play the odd game for the Foresters and MCC. In fact, it was whilst playing for the MCC in 1949 in the Scarborough Festival, he recorded his highest-ever first-class score of 156 not out against Yorkshire. In the two years he played for Lancashire, Cranston scored 1,928 runs at 40.16 and took 142 wickets at a cost of 23.00 runs each.

CRAWLEY, JOHN

Playing for Cambridge in 1991, John Crawley scored 83 for the University in the match against Lancashire and 66 and 59 not out in the Varsity match. Also that summer he scored his first century for Lancashire, 130 against Surrey at Old Trafford.

The following year, Crawley was appointed captain of the University side and scored a magnificent 106 in the Varsity match to lead his side to victory by seven wickets. He played in seven games for the county that summer, scoring 172 against Surrey at Lytham.

In 1993, Crawley in his last year for the University hit his highest score for the students, 187 not out against Sussex at Hove. In his three seasons at Fenners, he scored 1,988 runs at an average of 49.70. That summer also saw him play for England 'A' against Essex.

His first full season at Old Trafford was 1994 when he topped the county batting averages with 1,300 runs at 61.90 and a highest score of 281 not out against Somerset at Southport. These impressive performances led to him winning his first Test cap against the touring South Africans at Lord's.

He headed the Lancashire batting averages again in 1995 with 1,203 runs at 52.30 and in the match against Glamorgan at Old Trafford, scored 182 and 108 to register a century in each innings of the match.

In the summer of 1996, he scored his first Test hundred against Pakistan at the Oval and has now built the foundations for what many people believe will be an outstanding career in the game.

CROSFIELD, SYDNEY

Though he was born in Warrington, Sydney Crosfield was educated at an Army school in Surrey, Wimbledon School. He joined Lancashire in 1883 after playing his early cricket with Sefton. However, after being unable to break into the strong Lancashire batting line-up, he elected to play for Cheshire between 1885 and 1887.

A.N. Hornby's career seemed to be coming to an end and with Archie MacLaren finding his feet, the Lancashire Committee turned to Crosfield to captain the side during part of the 1892 and 1893 seasons. A solicitor by profession, Crosfield was also renown as a crack shot and won numerous competitions at the Manchester Gun Club.

Relieved of the captaincy for the 1894 season, Crosfield continued to play for the county and in 90 matches, scored 1,909 runs at an average of 15.03 and a top score of 82. He died in the Canary Isles in 1908 at the age of 46.

CUTTELL, WILLIS

After taking 106 wickets in 1895 and 95 in 1896 as professional for Nelson in the Lancashire League, Cuttell was given two games for the county in that latter season. Though he failed to impress, he was recalled the following summer to help Lancashire win the Championship outright for the first time in sixteen years.

In 1898, Cuttell became the first Lancashire player to accomplish the 'double' of 1,000 runs and 100 wickets and was selected as one of Wisden's 'Five Cricketers of the Year'. His performances during that campaign led to him being selected for C. Aubrey Smith's team to tour South Africa in the close season, where he played in both Tests.

His best performance with the ball for Lancashire came in that

W.R.CUTTELL,
LANCASHIRE.

summer of 1908 when he took eight for 105 against Gloucestershire at Old Trafford. In 1901 he took seven for 19 against Derbyshire and in 1904, four for 3 against Kent.

As a batsman, Cuttell hit five centuries for Lancashire with a top score of 137 against Nottinghamshire at Old Trafford in 1899. In 1906 when Cuttell was 41, he scored 95 batting at Number 9 in the match against Somerset and followed it with five wickets in the first innings.

In eleven seasons with Lancashire, Willis Cuttell, the son of an all-rounder who appeared for Yorkshire, scored 5,389 runs at an average of 20.41 and took 760 wickets at 19.59 runs apiece.

D

DEAN, HARRY

Spanning the years between 1906 and 1921, Harry Dean's career saw him take 1,267 wickets for Lancashire at 18.01 runs apiece. A left-arm swerve bowler, he could also bowl left-arm spin if the wicket suited it and was for a number of seasons, one of the best bowlers in the country. In 1907, his second season in the Lancashire team, he took 110 wickets, including nine for 46 against Derbyshire.

In 1909 he took nine for 31 against Warwickshire at Aigburth and then later that summer had match figures of fourteen for 77 against Somerset at Old Trafford. In 1911, Dean got through more overs and took more wickets than

H. DEAN,
LANCASHIRE.

any other bowler in the country. His 179 wickets for Lancashire costing 17.48 runs apiece. The following season he resorted to spin on the softer wickets and in the match against Kent at Old Trafford he had match figures of fifteen for 108, claiming his last wicket in the final over to give Lancashire victory.

It was during the summer of 1912 that the Burnley-born bowler made his Test debut, playing against Australia and South Africa in the Triangular Tournament.

In 1913, an extra Roses match was arranged at Aigburth as part of the celebrations to commemorate the visit of King George V. Lancashire beat Yorkshire by three wickets with Dean taking seventeen Yorkshire wickets for 92 runs.

Had the First World War not taken four seasons out of Dean's career, it is possible that he could have surpassed Johnny Briggs record total of 1,696 wickets for the county.

His benefit season of 1920 saw him take 124 wickets at 16.16 runs each with a best of eight for 80 against Surrey at Old Trafford. His career was drawing to a close and in 1921 after a season of indifferent form, he faded from the first-class scene.

DEBUTS

Four Lancashire cricketers have scored centuries on their first appearances for the county. They are:

1867	J. Ricketts v Surrey at the Oval	195*
1890	A.C. MacLaren v Sussex at Brighton	108
1908	R. Whitehead v Nottinghamshire at Old Trafford	131*
1990	G. Yates v Nottinghamshire at Trent Bridge	106 (on his Championship debut) (Batsman "not out" indicated by *)

Ken Cranston is the only Lancashire players since the Second World War to have made his England debut in his first-class debut season. This he did against South Africa in 1947.

DEFEATS

Lancashire's heaviest defeat came in 1950 when the West Indies beat them by an innings and 220 runs in the match at Old Trafford.

Lancashire's heaviest defeat in a County Championship match came at Old Trafford in 1938 when Yorkshire won by an innings and 200 runs.

DERBYSHIRE

Founded in 1870, Derbyshire's solitary Championship title came in 1936. The county also won the inaugural Nat West Bank Trophy tournament in 1981, the Sunday League in 1990 and the Benson and Hedges Trophy in 1993.

Derbyshire's first visit to Old Trafford in 1871 saw Lancashire bowled out for 25, which still stands as their lowest total against any county. When Lancashire visited Derby in 1888, the spectators jeered the former Derbyshire player, Frank Sugg. When he went in to bat, there was a noisy demonstration and when Hornby was at the wicket with him, the crowd became more abusive. So much so, the Lancashire captain left the field in disgust and offered to give up the match. After a delay of just over fifteen minutes, he was persuaded to continue playing, but the incident had left a sour taste in the mouth and Lancashire refused to play Derbyshire again for four years.

In 1899, Albert Ward was dismissed in a most unusual way in the match against Derbyshire. With his score on 72, he on-drove a ball from Davidson to the boundary but his bat splintered as he hit the ball and a piece fell on to his wickets and knocked off the bails.

In 1920, Lancashire's Lol Cook took seven wickets for eight runs with one of the finest pieces of skilled bowling in county cricket for many years.

In 1996 Jason Gallian scored 312 against Derbyshire at Old Trafford to set a new record for the highest score made by a Lancashire player at the County's headquarters.

Lancashire's record of first-class matches v Derbyshire is:

P.	W.	L.	D.	Tied
207	93	30	84	0

DOUBLE

The feat of scoring 1,000 runs and taking 100 wickets in a season has been performed four times by three Lancashire players:

		For Lancashire		All First-Class Games	
	Year	Runs	Wkts	Runs	Wkts
W.R. Cuttell	1898	952	109	1003	114
J. Hallows	1904	1071	108	1071	108
J.L. Hopwood	1934	1660	111	1672	111
J.L. Hopwood	1935	1538	103	1538	103

Johnny Briggs is the only cricketer who has scored 10,000 runs and taken 1,000 wickets for Lancashire, his complete figures being 10,707 runs and 1,696 wickets.

DOUBLE CENTURIES

J.T. Tyldesley has scored the most double centuries for Lancashire with thirteen between 1895 and 1923. In 1928, Frank Watson made three scores of over 200.

DUCKWORTH, GEORGE

George Duckworth first played for Lancashire in 1923 and was the county's first choice wicket-keeper until his retirement from first-class cricket at the end of the 1937 season, although he did make four further appearances when Farrimond was injured.

His best year behind the stumps for Lancashire was 1928 when he claimed 97 victims for the county with 69 caught and 28 stumped.

He made his Test debut for England in 1924 and appeared in 24 Tests, touring Australia three times. The Warrington-born wicket-keeper was renown for his shrill appeals and it was once said of him on a tour 'Down Under' that when he appealed in Sydney, an umpire was liable to give a batsman out in Melbourne!

In his career for the county he helped dismiss 922 batsmen (634 caught and 288 stumped). When he took off his pads for the last time, he started a new career as a radio and television commentator and acted as baggage master on a number of MCC overseas tours and for several sides visiting England. The popular wicket-keeper served on the Lancashire Committee, surviving the 1964 upheaval before passing away two years later.

DURHAM

Founded in 1882, Durham entered the County Championship in 1992, when the counties met for the first time at Gateshead Fell. Replying to Durham's 312 all out, Lancashire scored 562 with Mike Atherton scoring a career best 199 in 500 minutes. Peter Martin coming in as a night-watchman scored his maiden first-class century and helped Atherton add 243 for the seventh wicket, only two runs short of the county record set in 1912. Lancashire won by 10 wickets and have won each of the five Championship games played.

In the Old Trafford meeting of 1993, Durham scored 515 for nine declared in their first innings but were then dismissed for 83 as Lancashire went on to win.

Lancashire's record of first-class matches v Durham is:

P.	W.	L.	D.	Tied
5	5	0	0	0

E

EAST LANCASHIRE

The East Lancashire Cricket Club was formed in 1863-64 on Alexandra Meadows, Blackburn, by the Officers of the 2nd Lancashire Rifle Volunteers.

In 1868 the Australian Aboriginal XI visited the ground to play the club and stumps were drawn with the home side still needing two runs to win with nine wickets in hand. In July 1875, there was a visit from Casey's Clown Cricketers and the Club still has a poster advertising the fixture.

The Club held its opening first-class match in May 1932 when Lancashire played Glamorgan but no play was possible after tea on the first day due to heavy rain. In 1933 Lancashire beat Worcestershire by an innings and 96 runs with Frank Watson scoring 186 and later that year, Northamptonshire were defeated by an innings and 74 runs, with both Paynter and Iddon scoring hundreds. In 1935, Glamorgan returned but brought the rain with them thus limiting play to under six hours and preventing a ball being bowled on the third day. No other first-class matches have been played on the ground but a number of Second Eleven matches have been played there.

ECKERSLEY, PETER

Though he made his Lancashire debut in 1923 it wasn't until Leonard Green took over the captaincy in 1926 that Eckersley gained a regular place in what turned out to be a Championship-winning side. That season his highest score was 99 but he impressed when called on to captain the side in Green's absence.

It was Eckersley who led the side in the title clinching match against Nottinghamshire at Aigburth. The following summer, he scored his maiden first-class century against Gloucestershire at Bristol and in the winter toured Jamaica with Lionel Tennyson's side. Unfortunately, he developed appendicitis and had to miss the entire 1928 season.

When he returned in 1929, it was as Lancashire captain, replacing Green who had retired. The Lowton-born batsman led the county to runners-up spot in his first season in charge and then in 1930, led the county to its fourth Championship in five seasons.

Eckersley was known as the 'cricketing airman' and often flew his own plane to matches. In 1935 he arranged the first-ever flight to take a cricket team to a match when two planes took Lancashire from Cardiff to Southampton in 51 minutes!

Despite Lancashire losing players of the calibre of Makepeace, Watson, Hallows, McDonald and Dick Tyldesley, Eckersley led the county to sixth in 1931 and 1932 and fifth in 1933. In 1934 he captained Lancashire to the Championship again but he was now showing a keen interest in politics and stood as a National Candidate for Leigh, though without success.

The 1935 season was his last for the county for in November of that year he was returned as Member of Parliament for the Exchange

Division of Manchester. Though he could have claimed exemption on the grounds of being a Member of Parliament, he joined the Air Arm of the RNVR and was tragically killed in a flying accident at Eastleigh in Hampshire in August 1940.

EDRICH, GEOFF

One of four first-class cricketing brothers, Geoff Edrich played for Norfolk prior to the Second World War, impressing with his attractive stroke-play and close to the wicket fielding. During the hostilities, he was taken Prisoner-of-War and when he was freed in August 1945, he weighed just six and a half stones. The following year, both Geoff and his brother Eric signed for Lancashire although Geoff had been approached by Hampshire prior to the outbreak of war.

Geoff Edrich played for Lancashire until 1958, scoring 14,730 runs at 34.74 with a top score of 167 against Nottinghamshire at Trent Bridge in 1954. He also topped 1,000 runs a season on eight occasions, with a best of 1,977 in 1952. In 1953-54, he toured India with the Commonwealth team and scored hundreds against Hyderabad and the Combined Universities.

In 1956, he was given the opportunity of captaining the county and of the ten matches in which he led the side, six were won. One of them being the match in which Lancashire defeated Leicestershire at Old Trafford without losing a wicket. He left the county in 1958 to play Minor Counties cricket for Cumberland and coach schoolchildren.

ENGINEER, FAROKH

Reading Advanced Economics and Commerce before taking a degree and graduating in accountancy and auditing, Farokh Engineer made his debut in representative cricket whilst at Bombay University. He played for the Combined Universities against the touring West Indies in 1958-59 and then for Bombay before winning his first cap for India in 1961.

He joined Lancashire on an immediate registration in 1968 but in that first season, rarely demonstrated the fine batting qualities that had persuaded the county to engage him as a wicket-keeper/batsman.

In 1969, he failed by only 48 runs to score 1,000 for the season, a feat he would most certainly have achieved if he had not missed four games due to a foot injury. That summer, he scored his first century for the county, hitting 103 against Glamorgan at Swansea and held eight catches in the match against Somerset at Taunton.

Farokh Engineer

A swashbuckling batsman, he narrowly missed the fastest televised fifty in the Sunday League match against Derbyshire at Buxton and in the same competition against Glamorgan at Southport in 1969, he scored an unbeaten 78 as Lancashire reached 113 for victory. However, in the County Championship he had to wait until 1975 before he scored his first hundred at Old Trafford, it coming in the match against Warwickshire.

For India, he played in 46 Tests, scoring 2,611 runs at 31.08 and recorded 82 dismissals (66 caught, 16 stumped).

ESSEX

Founded in 1876, Essex went 103 years without winning a major trophy, but made up with this with eleven titles between 1979 and 1996. They have won the Championship on six occasions (1979, 1983, 1984, 1986, 1991 and 1992), the Benson and Hedges Cup in 1979, the Nat West Bank Trophy in 1985 and the Sunday League in 1981, 1984 and 1985.

In 1897 after a ten year gap, Lancashire resumed games with Essex. On a wearing wicket at Leyton, Lancashire were in trouble, but when it looked as if they would follow on, leaving Essex to bat last, Fred Bull, the home side's off-break bowler bowled one ball so wide that it went for four runs. Arthur Mold then decided to hit his own wicket to make sure Lancashire followed-on! Hornby refused to carry on with the game but after Bull apologised for his antics, the game continued.

When the two teams met at Colchester in 1928, Lancashire bowled Essex out for a second time at 6.25pm on the second day and needed just two runs for victory. The players had to return the following morning for what turned out to be two balls. George Eastman, Essex's wicket-keeper didn't bother to wear pads, Johnny Douglas wore plus fours, while many other Essex players wore ordinary clothes!

In 1996 Glen Chapple produced a remarkable spell of bowling to take six for 18 in the Nat West Trophy Final at Lord's to give Lancashire victory over Essex by 129 runs.

Lancashire's record of first-class matches v Essex is:

P.	W.	L.	D.	Tied
137	44	29	63	1

F

FAIRBROTHER, NEIL

After coming to the county's notice while playing for Grappenhall in the Manchester Association, Neil Fairbrother made his Lancashire debut against Kent in 1982. He did not bat in that game but in his debut innings against Warwickshire at Edgbaston the following season, he was on 94 when Lancashire had reached 250, the total skipper Abrahams had agreed to declare on.

Since then, the dashing left-hander has more than made up for it with over 15,000 runs and 35 centuries. His highest score of 366 came against Surrey at the Oval in 1990 as he and Mike Atherton put 364 on for Lancashire's third wicket.

In the month of May that summer, he scored exactly 1,000 runs in all competitions – 674 in the County Championship, 201 in the Benson and Hedges Cup and 125 in the Refuge Assurance Sunday League.

Neil Fairbrother

The following season, he hit hundreds in three successive innings and in 1992 and 1993 he captained the county. His form wasn't affected in his first season in charge but 1993 was an unhappy year for him, hitting his only century for the county in September.

Fairbrother's Test record of 219 runs at 15.64 is certainly not a true reflection of his abilities. His first four Test appearances brought him just five runs, though he did later play a fine innings of 83 against India in Madras. He has played in 51 one-day internationals and included among his 1,451 runs was a superb innings of 113 against the West Indies at Lord's in 1991.

A magnificent striker of the ball, he has recently signed a new contract with Lancashire that will keep him at Old Trafford until the turn of the century.

FALLOWS, JACK

The son of the then treasurer J.C. Fallows, Jack Fallows was 39 years of age when he was appointed Lancashire captain in 1946. Though he lacked first-class experience, he did score 135 when captaining the Manchester side pre-war, the name the Club and Ground XI played under in the 1930s.

Fallows was an Army officer, popular with his men and more than willing to attempt the task of captaining the county. Lancashire were not an easy side to captain but Fallows found a solution to all his problems and on many occasions showed a real flair for the job. One of these occasions was against Nottinghamshire at Old Trafford when a snap declaration brought victory for the Red-Rose side, another was his use of Jack Ikin against Surrey when there were far too few runs to gamble with.

A straightforward, attacking batsman, his top score in his only season with the county was 35 in the match against Yorkshire at Old Trafford.

FARRIMOND, BILL

Wicket-keeper Bill Farrimond was kept out of the Lancashire side by George Duckworth, though in 1930-31, he toured South Africa with England and kept wicket in the last two Tests at Johannesburg and Durban. Farrimond also played in the second Test against the West Indies at Port of Spain in 1935 and made the last of his four Test appearances later that year against South Africa at Lord's.

For Lancashire, he was the regular wicket-keeper only for the last two seasons prior to the outbreak of the Second World War, claiming 333 victims. (256 caught and 77 stumped). In 1930, he caught six and stumped one during Kent's second innings in the match at Old Trafford.

Though he had joined Lancashire in 1924, he only played in a handful of matches when Duckworth was injured or on international duty. However, in his later seasons, Duckworth often stepped down to give Farrimond more experience. During the war years, Farrimond returned to his native Westhoughton and played in the Bolton League side which won the championship in four consecutive seasons from 1940 to 1943.

FASTEST HUNDRED

In 1983, Steve O'Shaughnessy equalled Percy Fender's time for the fastest first-class hundred. It was equalled in bizarre circumstances. He opened Lancashire's second innings with Graeme Fowler at Old Trafford shortly before 3.00pm. on 13 September, the final afternoon of that season. After Leicestershire had scored 150 to gain the batting point they needed to secure fourth place, they declared 86 runs adrift of Lancashire's total in the hope of beings set a target.

The bowlers sent down a succession of full-tosses and long-hops which the Lancashire openers initially blocked in protest. The batsmen then began an assault which saw O'Shaughnessy register his second first-class hundred in 35 minutes (off at least 8 balls more than Fender required). His innings included 5 sixes and 17 fours. His partnership of 201 in 43 minutes with Fowler is the fastest double-century stand on record.

FATHERS AND SONS

There have been 12 instances of fathers and sons representing Lancashire. A.N. Hornby, one of the greatest figures in the history of Lancashire County Cricket Club, captained the side between 1880 and 1891, shared the captaincy during 1892 and 1893 and returned for a third spell in 1897-98. During this time, Lancashire won the County Championship outright for the first time. His son, A.H. Hornby, followed father as a Lancashire player and captain. He was the sixth captain to be officially elected and found his father as the Club's President during his time in charge.

David Lloyd captained Lancashire between 1973 and 1977 and led the side to success in the 1975 Gillette Cup Final against Middlesex. In 1974 he appeared in the first of his nine Tests and celebrated with a magnificent innings of 214 not out against India at Edgbaston. His son Graham Lloyd made his Lancashire debut in 1988 and in 1996 made his first appearance for England in a one-day international when they beat Pakistan at Old Trafford.

FIFTIES

The record for the most fifties in consecutive first-class innings was set by Ernest Tyldesley with ten in succession between 26 June and 27 July 1926. His sequence was as follows:

144	v Warwickshire at Edgbaston
69	v Kent at Dover
144*	v Kent at Dover
226	v Sussex at Old Trafford
51	v Surrey at The Oval
131	v Surrey at The Oval
131	v Gentlemen (for Players) at Lord's
106	v Essex at Leyton
126	v Somerset at Taunton
81	v Australia (for England) at Old Trafford

FINALS

Lancashire have appeared in the following limited-overs finals.

Year	Opponents	Competition	Result
1970	Sussex	Gillette Cup	Won by 6 wickets
1971	Kent	Gillette Cup	Won by 24 runs
1972	Warwickshire	Gillette Cup	Won by 4 wickets
1974	Kent	Gillette Cup	Lost by 4 wickets
1975	Middlesex	Gillette Cup	Won by 7 wickets
1976	Northamptonshire	Gillette Cup	Lost by 4 wickets
1984	Warwickshire	Benson and Hedges	Won by 6 wickets
1986	Sussex	Nat West Trophy	Lost by 7 wickets
1988	Worcestershire	Refuge Assurance	Won by 52 runs
1990	Worcestershire	Benson and Hedges	Won by 69 runs
1990	Northamptonshire	Nat West Trophy	Won by 7 wickets

1991	Worcestershire	Refuge Assurance	Lost by 7 runs
1991	Worcestershire	Benson and Hedges	Lost by 65 runs
1993	Derbyshire	Benson and Hedges	Lost by 6 runs
1995	Kent	Benson and Hedges	Won by 35 runs
1996	Northamptonshire	Benson and Hedges	Won by 31 runs
1996	Essex	Nat West Trophy	Won by 129 runs

FIRST COUNTY MATCH

Lancashire's first inter-county match was played at Old Trafford on 20,21,22 July 1865. The visitors were Middlesex who were beaten by 62 runs despite the feats of the Walker brothers.

Lancashire batted first and scored 243 runs. Middlesex then proceeded to compile exactly the same total, thanks to R.D. Walker who scored 84. Lancashire's second innings of 178 provided V.E. Walker with all ten wickets. Middlesex then collapsed to 116 all out with the two Walker brothers scoring 57 of the runs.

FOOTBALLERS

There have been a number of Lancashire cricketers who have been footballers of real note. A.N. 'Monkey' Hornby played for Blackburn Rovers, whilst his famous opening partner, Richard Barlow refereed the FA Cup tie between Preston North End and Hyde, when the Lilywhites won 26-0. Frank Sugg who scored 9,620 runs for the county, captained Sheffield Wednesday and Burnley and also played for Bolton Wanderers.

In 1906, the Everton team that beat Newcastle United 1-0 in the FA Cup Final, had England internationals Jack Sharp and Harry Makepeace in their ranks. Sharp who won two caps for England, appeared in three Tests, whilst Makepeace, who was capped four times at football played in four Tests for England. Both players scored hundreds, Sharp 105 v Australia at the Oval in 1909 and Makepeace 117 v Australia at Melbourne in 1921.

Fast bowler Gordon Hodgson, who took 148 wickets for Lancashire at 27.75 runs apiece, played for Liverpool, Aston Villa and Leeds United, whilst Fred Goodwin who appeared for Manchester United in the 1958 FA Cup Final against Bolton Wanderers appeared in 11 games for the county.

Also around this time, Peter Greenwood appeared for Chester and Ken Higgs, who captured 1,033 wickets at 22.90 played for Port Vale.

Australian-born Ken Grieves, who scored 20,802 runs and took 235 wickets and also holds the county record for the most catches with 555, kept goal for Stockport County, Bury and Bolton Wanderers.

In the 1956 FA Cup Final, all-rounder Jack Dyson scored Manchester City's goal in their 3-1 defeat by Birmingham City.

The last Lancashire player to play League football was Jim Cumbes who kept goal for Tranmere Rovers, West Bromwich Albion and Aston Villa.

FORMATION

The first steps in forming a County Cricket Club were taken at a meeting held in the Queen's Hotel, Manchester, on 12 January 1864, when after "a thorough discussion of the possibilities and desirability of spreading a thorough knowledge and appreciation of the game throughout Lancashire" it was decided to go ahead and form a County Cricket Club. It was agreed that matches should be played in Manchester, Blackburn, Liverpool and Preston and "other places where interest was manifest". It was also resolved that the annual subscription of members should be one guinea and that any profit would be used to fund and maintain a ground that would meet all the cricketing requirements of Lancashire County Cricket Club.

FOWLER, GRAEME

After playing for the Lancashire 2nd XI at the age of 16, Graeme Fowler went on to represent the English Schools Cricket Association, MCC Schools and Young England as a wicket-keeper/ batsman. In 1976 he was selected as the Lancashire Cricket Federation Young Cricketer of the Year and after leaving Durham University, he joined Lancashire full-time. He made his county debut against Derbyshire in 1979 and the following summer made the first of 29 centuries for the county, when he hit 106 not out against Nottinghamshire at Old Trafford.

Graeme Fowler

In 1982, he made his Test debut against Pakistan, top scoring with 86 in England's second innings. Also that summer he hit two centuries in the match against Warwickshire at Southport, both scored with the aid of a runner.

He scored his first Test century against New Zealand at the Oval in 1983, the summer he scored a century in 46 minutes against Leicestershire at Old Trafford. The following season, he made the top score of his career, 226 against Kent at Maidstone and then touring India in 1984-85 he scored 201 in the Madras Test. He followed this with an innings of 69 at Kanpur but was then promptly dropped! His 21 Test appearances brought him 1,307 runs at an average of 35.32.

His limited-overs performances for Lancashire have been superb and in 1990, he scored 773 runs in the Sunday League, a record for Lancashire. He has scored hundreds in all three major one-day competitions and holds the county record for the highest score in the Benson and Hedges Cup.

At the end of the 1992 season, Fowler was released after scoring 13,453 runs at 36.55 and joined Durham. One of Lancashire's most popular players, he is currently based at Durham University's Cricket Centre of Excellence.

G

GHOST!

Cecil Parkin ended his Test career when he published a criticism of his captain's management of the bowling. After Tate and Gilligan had dismissed South Africa at Edgbaston for 30, they made 309 when following on and Parkin only bowled 16 overs.

He, or more probably, his ghost, wrote a piece in a newspaper suggesting that he ought to have been used more and he was not picked again.

GILLETTE CUP

The first inter-county limited overs competition competed for by all the first-class counties and sponsored by Gillette started in 1963. The opening match was a preliminary round between Lancashire and Leicestershire at Old Trafford. Scheduled to be played on 1 May, rain delayed the start and the match was completed the following day.

In their then 65 overs, Lancashire scored 304 for nine with Peter Marner scoring 121. Leicestershire replied with 203 all out, Lancashire thus becoming the first team to win a match in the competition.

Lancashire won the Gillette Cup four times and a further two times when Nat West took over the sponsorship in 1981. Their results in those four finals were as follows:

1970	Sussex 184	Lancashire 185 for four
1971	Lancashire 224 for seven	Kent 200
1972	Warwickshire 234	Lancashire 235 for six
1975	Middlesex 180	Lancashire 182 for three

Lancashire also appeared in two other finals when Gillette sponsored the competition in 1974 and 1976.

In the semi-final of the 1971 competition on 28 July, Gloucestershire set Lancashire 230 to win. Thanks to David Hughes in the dark of Old Trafford at 9.00pm. the Red-Rose county won by three wickets.

A packed Lord's saw a magnificent final in 1971. Lancashire's 224 for seven was protected by a superb display of fielding which backed

The Lancashire side that reached the 1974 final of the Gillette Cup:
J. Sullivan, K. Shuttleworth, P. Lee, C. Lloyd, F. Engineer, F. Hayes, K. Goodwin, J. Simmons
P. Lever, K. Snellgrove, D. Lloyd (Captain), H. Pilling, D. Hughes, B. Wood

up some accurate bowling. Lancashire's captain Jack Bond showed the influence he was able to exert on the side by bringing off an unbelievable catch to dismiss Asif Iqbal as he threatened to win the match for Kent.

The following year, Clive Lloyd showed the sell-out crowd at Lord's his greatness, by scoring a magnificent 126 as he steered Lancashire to a four-wicket win. Lancashire's full record in the Gillette Cup is as follows:

P.	W.	L.
53	39	14

Other Gillette Cup records include:

Highest Innings Total	304 for 9 v Leicestershire at Old Trafford in 1963.
Lowest Completed Innings	59 v Worcestershire at Worcester in 1963.

Highest Individual Score	131 by A. Kennedy v Middlesex at Old Trafford in 1978.
Best Bowling Performance	5 for 28 by B. Statham v Leicestershire at Old Trafford in 1963.
Highest Partnership	234 for 4th wicket by D. Lloyd and C. Lloyd v Gloucestershire at Old Trafford in 1963
Man of the Match Award	6 by C. Lloyd and B. Wood

GLAMORGAN

Founded in 1888, Glamorgan have twice won the Championship, in 1948 and 1969. The county also won the Sunday League in 1993.

Cec Parkin produced some amazing bowling in the match against Glamorgan at Aigburth in 1924. Lancashire themselves had been dismissed for 49 and the Welsh side smelt victory. Parkin had other ideas as he took the first six wickets to fall for the cost of just one run. Two of his victims were caught in the deep, two by Dick Tyldesley at short leg, one bowled and one caught and bowled, when he threw the ball high into the air and caught it behind his back. He finished with six for six and with Dick Tyldesley taking four for 16, Glamorgan were all out for 22, the lowest total made against Lancashire. The home side went on to win the game by 128 runs. Lancashire's record of first-class matches v Glamorgan is:

P.	W.	L.	D.	Tied
115	36	18	61	0

GLOUCESTERSHIRE

Founded in 1871, Gloucestershire won the unofficial County Championship in 1874, 1876 and 1877 and were joint champions in 1873. Since 1930, the county has finished second in the Championship on six occasions. Gloucestershire have had two one-day successes, winning the Gillette Cup in 1973 and the Benson and Hedges Cup in 1977.

In 1878, Lancashire played Gloucestershire at Old Trafford, fielding what was regarded then as their best ever team. The Gloucestershire side contained W.G. Grace and his brothers E.M. and G.F, along with their cousin Walter Gilbert and Bill Midwinter, who W.G. had persuaded to leave the Australian team who were touring the country, midway through their visit. In a rain interrupted first day, Lancashire finished on 88 for nine but within minutes of the start of the second, were all out for 89, Barlow first man in, was last out for 40. Gloucestershire were then bowled out for 116, a lead of 27 on the first innings. A.N. Hornby scored 100 in Lancashire's second innings total of 262, leaving Gloucestershire to score 236 for victory. They ended on 125 for five, but as Gloucestershire were the Champion County, this was deemed the turning point in Lancashire's history, for three years later, they won their first County Championship.

In 1880 in the match at Clifton, Lancashire scored 186 and had Gloucestershire at 58 for five at the end of the first day. But then W.G. Grace hit his only hundred of the summer, enabling the home side to total 249. Lancashire collapsed to 85 in their second innings, Gloucestershire winning by seven wickets.

During the match at Old Trafford in 1887, a Gloucestershire fielder named Arthur Croome chased after a lofty hit from Lancashire wicket-keeper Dick Pilling. He missed the ball, fell over the surrounding railings and one of the spikes entered his neck just below the chin. He was attended to by Gloucestershire's famous doctors W.G and E.M. Grace and assisted by Dr Royle, they stitched the wound. Croome took no further part in a game which Lancashire won by an innings and 98 runs.

The game against Gloucestershire at Old Trafford in 1925 saw Jack Sharp at the age of 47, captain Lancashire for the last time. The game saw the highest partnership against Lancashire at Old Trafford as Alf Dipper and Wally Hammond shared a stand of 330 runs in 223 minutes for the third wicket. Dipper scored 144 but it was the 20-year-old Hammond, who scored 250 not out, reaching this score with a massive six off Dick Tyldesley that rested in the upper tier of the pavilion.

The Gillette Cup semi-final of 1971 played at Old Trafford in front of the television cameras saw Gloucestershire score 229 for six in their sixty overs. Lancashire needed 27 to win in six overs with Mike Procter still to bowl when David Hughes walked to the wicket. It was almost a quarter to nine, but in the 56th over, Hughes attacked off-spinner John Mortimore, hitting him for 24 runs. Lancashire needed one to win and Bond edged Procter to give the Red-Rose county a famous victory. Lancashire's record of first-class matches v Gloucestershire is:

P.	W.	L.	D.	Tied
173	79	27	67	0

GREEN, LEONARD

After making his county debut in 1922, Green scored what turned out

OGDEN'S CIGARETTES.

MAJOR L. GREEN,
LANCASHIRE.

to be his only Championship century the following season when he stood in as captain for the injured Jack Sharp.

When Sharp stood down at the end of the 1925 season, Leonard Green was the natural successor and in his first season in charge, led Lancashire to their first Championship success for 22 years. He was a firm disciplinarian and being a Major in the First World War, was masterly in the command of the men who played for him. His was leadership of the highest quality and though it was occasionally suggested that his batting left a lot to be desired, he was never found wanting in a crisis.

He led Lancashire to the Championship title again in 1927 and 1928 and in this latter season, Lancashire did not lose a single match. At the end of the 1928 season, he gave way to business demands, although he did play in a further 11 games over the next seven seasons.

GREENHOUGH, TOMMY

Tommy Greenhough made his first-class debut for Lancashire in July 1951 against Hampshire and went on to play in 241 matches for the county in a fifteen year career at Old Trafford.

In spite of a succession of niggling injuries, the Rochdale-born spinner took 707 wickets for Lancashire at a cost of 21.98 runs apiece.

He played in four Tests for England and in his second at Lord's against India, he helped dismiss the tourists for 168 in their first innings by taking five for 12 in 31 balls. His final figures in that innings were five for 35 but if Godfrey Evans hadn't missed four stumpings within the space of fifteen minutes, who knows what his analysis might have been!

In 1959, a season in which 23 batsmen scored over 2,000 runs each, Greenhough took 93 wickets at 22 runs each, a really good performance. In 1959-60, he toured the Caribbean and though he took six for 32 in the opening match against the Windward Islands and took more wickets than anyone except Allen and Trueman, he failed to make the Test team.

Returning to Lancashire, he had a magnificent season in 1960, taking 111 wickets at 18.23 runs apiece and won his place back in the England side against South Africa at The Oval. However, it proved to be Greenhough's final appearance at international level and in 1966 after losing much of his pace and bounce he parted company with the county.

GRIEVES, KEN

Sydney-born Ken Grieves proved to be one of Lancashire's best post-war all-round cricketers. He made his debut for New South Wales in 1945-46 and in only his third first-class match, scored a century against the Australian Services.

He had played for two seasons with Rawtenstall before joining Lancashire in 1949. In only his second game for the county, he scored 68 and 91 and took eight wickets in the match against Somerset at Old Trafford. The first of his 26 centuries came against Oxford University in his fourth match and by the end of the season, he had scored 1,047 runs, the fourth player to score 1,000 runs in his first season.

In 1950, he held the county's middle-order batting together as Lancashire shared the title with Surrey and at the end of the season, he went on the Commonwealth tour of India and Ceylon, scoring centuries in both matches against the Governors XI.

A world-class slip fielder, he broke the county record for the most outfield catches in a season in 1950 with 63 and a year later equalled Dick Tyldesley's feat of holding six catches in an innings against Sussex at Old Trafford.

In 1957, he scored a career best 224 against Cambridge University and in 1959 he scored 2,253 runs for the county. In 1962, he decided to give up the county game and returned to the Leagues as professional for Stockport in the Central Lancashire League.

However, in 1963 he was lured back to Old Trafford as Lancashire's captain but after two years in charge, he was one of four players released for the 1965 season.

He played in 452 matches for Lancashire, scoring 20,802 runs at 33.39 and taking 235 wickets at 28.80 runs apiece, but it is for his brilliant fielding that he is best remembered, with the popular Australian holding the county record with 555 catches.

GROUNDSMEN

The first groundsman of note was Fred Reynolds, who had played in Lancashire's first match in 1865. He took part in 38 games, taking ninety-four wickets at 19.39 runs each. His staff consisted of one boy and a horse to pull both the roller and the cutter, yet he still managed to produces wickets that not only looked good, but played well. Fred Reynolds also served behind the bar and his wife saw to it that the pavilion was always spick and span.

Tom Matthews followed Reynolds in 1908 and unknown to him, he addressed some uncomplimentary remarks to top brass from Lord's who were inspecting the wicket prior to a vital game, telling them in no uncertain terms to keep off the grass!

Arthur Widdowson was the first Lancashire groundsman to 'mechanise' the job of ground preparation. He placed great faith in a special kind of marl, enabling him to prepare the perfect batting wickets. A perfectionist, he could often be seen in the outfield on his hands and knees uprooting the occasional daisy roots. It was also Widdowson who lodged a complaint about 'Parkin and Tyldesley's ruination of the square' after the bowlers had dug out a large lump of turf in their efforts to obtain a satisfactory foot-hold in a rain-affected match.

Around this time, former Lancashire all-rounder John I'Anson, who scored 986 runs and took 148 wickets for the county left Old Trafford and went to be Head Gardener on the Duke of Westminster's estate at Eaton Park.

Harry Williams who could always be found with his dog 'Trafford' at his heels, was the groundsman who attended to the damage done in World War Two. Not even a bomb crater some six feet deep could provide a problem for Harry Williams.

No groundsman worked harder than Bert Flack, not only in mastering the art of preparing pitches, but in resuscitating them from the heavy rain synonymous with Old Trafford.

In recent years, Lancashire's Head Groundsman Peter Marron has been voted Groundsman of the Year on a number of occasions.

H

HALLOWS, CHARLIE

For eleven seasons between 1919 and 1930, Charlie Hallows exceeded 1,000 runs and in 1925, 1927 and 1928 he made over two thousand runs. Between making his debut in 1914 and playing the last of his 370 matches in 1932, Hallows scored 20,142 runs for the county at 39.72 and scored 52 centuries.

WILLS'S CIGARETTES.

C. HALLOWS.

His best year was 1928 when he scored 2,564 runs at 65.74 and achieved a permanent place in cricket records when he scored a thousand runs in the month of May. One of a select group of three batsmen to achieve this feat, he scored his runs at a better average than Grace or Hammond.

In 1929, he carried his bat through the Lancashire innings in the Roses match at Old Trafford in making 152 not out, a superb innings lasting over seven hours.

A fine county batsman, Hallows only played in two Tests for England, the first against Australia in 1921 and then against the West Indies seven years later.

He played a significant part in the county's three successive Championship victories of 1926, 1927 and 1928 and in this latter season, shared with Frank Watson in twelve stands of over 100, five of them double centuries.

After his playing career was over, he held professional engagements for a number of clubs before becoming coach at Worcestershire. He later returned to Old Trafford as Lancashire's Chief Coach but failed to achieve the same success he had at New Road.

HAMPSHIRE

Founded in 1863, Hampshire have twice won the County Championship first under the enthusiastic captaincy of Colin Ingleby-Mackenzie in 1961 and again in 1973, by which time their captain was
Richard Gilliat. The county have won the Sunday League on three
occasions – 1975, 1978 and 1986, the Benson and Hedges Cup in 1988
and 1992 and the Nat West Trophy in 1991.

When Lancashire met Hampshire in 1870, A.N. Hornby scored 132
and was presented with a bat, but an even more unusual performance
was that of Bill Hickton, who became the first Lancashire player to
take all ten wickets in an innings – ten for 46.

When Lancashire played Hampshire in 1911, they scored 621 for
six on the opening day, which was then the third highest score made
in a day in a county match. Spooner scored 102 before lunch and
went on to score 186, Sharp hit 135, whilst MacLeod was allowed to
reach his hundred the following day.

The match against Hampshire in 1920 provided a thrilling finish
after the southern county had needed only 66 for victory. With just
13 runs required and seven wickets in hand, it all looked so easy.
Then four wickets fell for the addition of just one run and when Lol
Cook bowled Greig, Hampshire were 57 for eight. The ninth wicket
fell at 60 and after taking a single, Frank Ryan hit Harry Dean to leg
for three runs. The next ball lifted sharply and Alex Kennedy was
forced to edge it to Boddington the Lancashire wicket-keeper. The
Red-Rose county had won by one run! Lancashire's record of first-
class matches v Hampshire is:

P.	W.	L.	D.	Tied
123	55	18	49	1

HAT-TRICKS

For the first time since the opening Roses game at Whalley in 1867,
Lancashire took a county game away from Old Trafford in 1876, when
Castleton near Rochdale staged the match against Kent. Lancashire
won by 10 wickets with Alec Watson taking seven for 61 in the second
innings, including the first hat-trick for Lancashire.

Richard Barlow and Ted McDonald have both performed the feat
on three occasions as has Brian Statham if his achievement for the

MCC v Transvaal at Johannesburg during the 1956-57 tour is included.

In 1968, Ken Higgs became the first Lancashire bowler to perform the hat-trick against Yorkshire.

Arthur Mold, Walter Brearley and Dick Tyldesley have all taken four wickets in four balls, whilst the last Lancashire player to perform the hat-trick was Mike Watkinson in the match against Warwickshire at Edgbaston in 1992.

HAYES, FRANK

After studying at Sheffield University, Frank Hayes joined Lancashire

Frank Hayes

in 1970 and after scoring 202 against Warwickshire 2nd XI, he was called up to the first team. In his first innings in the County Championship, he had made 94 against Middlesex when he tried to reach his hundred a with lofted drive, only to be caught at deep mid-on. In his second match for the county against Hampshire he made 99 before being stumped and it seemed that it would only be a matter of time before he reached three figures in the Championship.

As it turned out, he lost form and it was 1973 before he scored his maiden first-class century, 100 not out against Sussex at Hove. Three days later he followed it with a magnificent innings of 154 against Glamorgan at Swansea and another hundred in the match against Nottinghamshire to make it his third in successive matches for the county.

He made his Test debut against the West Indies at the Oval later that summer and hit a brilliant 106 not out in the second innings to become the first Lancashire player to score a century on his Test debut.

In 1974, he scored what was to be his highest score for the county, 187 against the touring Indians and the following season hit his first hundred in Roses matches. In 1977 he hit Glamorgan bowler Malcolm Nash for 34 in one over with five 6's and a four, so nearly emulating Gary Sobers' feat of 36 in an over off the same bowler!

Frank Hayes captained Lancashire from 1978 to 1980 but after suffering a series of niggling injuries retired on medical advice after playing in the opening fixture of the 1984 season. He had scored 10,899 runs for the county at an average of 37.45 and scored 23 centuries.

HICKTON, BILL

Derbyshire-born Bill Hickton played in just 24 matches for Lancashire between 1867 and 1871, taking 144 wickets at a cost of 14.05 runs each. He was the first Lancashire bowler to take all ten wickets in an innings when he took ten for 46 in the match against Hampshire at Old Trafford in 1870, to finish with match figures of fourteen for 73.

In 1871 he returned to his native county and played against Lancashire in their first match, producing match figures of seven for 74, as Derbyshire won by an innings. He also played for Lancashire that year, turning out in the county's four remaining games against Kent and Yorkshire.

HIGGS, KEN

Following National Service, Staffordshire-born Ken Higgs made his debut for Lancashire in 1958 in the match against Hampshire. It was a remarkable debut performance by the young bowler, who took seven for 36 in nine overs to give Lancashire an easy target for victory. He ended that first season with 66 wickets, a most commendable performance.

Years of consistent fast bowling eventually brought Higgs his Test debut for England against South Africa at the Oval in 1965. Partnering Brian Statham, he finished with match figures of eight for 143. He appeared in fifteen Tests, taking 71 wickets at 20.74 runs apiece and shared with John Snow in a tenth-wicket partnership of 128 against the West Indies at the Oval in 1966.

After a disagreement with the Lancashire Committee, Higgs left Old Trafford at the end of the 1969 season after taking 1,033 wickets at 22.90 runs each. He played for a couple of seasons with Rishton in the Lancashire League before in 1972, Leicestershire persuaded him to return to the first-class game.

He had taken seven for 19, his best career figures against Leicester-

shire in 1965, so it was hardly surprising that they headed the list of counties eager to acquire his services. He was still very fit and even after being appointed Leicestershire's coach, he came out of retirement in 1986 at the age of 49 to take five for 22 against Yorkshire!

He always enjoyed his batting and in 1977, he and Ray Illingworth added 228 for the last wicket against Northamptonshire. Higgs was on 98 when he ran himself out, though he tended to take the view that his more elderly partner was at fault!

Ken Higgs

HIGHEST INDIVIDUAL SCORES

The top individual scores by Lancashire players are as follows:

424	A.C. MacLaren	v Somerset at Taunton	1895
366	N.H. Fairbrother	v Surrey at The Oval	1990
322	E. Paynter	v Sussex at Hove	1937
312	J. Gallian	v Derbyshire at Old Trafford	1996
300*	F. Watson	v Surrey at Old Trafford	1928
295*	J.T. Tyldesley	v Kent at Old Trafford	1906
291	E. Paynter	v Hampshire at Southampton	1938
272	J.T. Tyldesley	v Derbyshire at Chesterfield	1919
266*	W. Place	v Oxford University at Oxford	1947
266	E. Paynter	v Essex at Old Trafford	1937

HIGHEST INNINGS

The highest individual score in first-class cricket by a Lancashire player is 424 by Archie MacLaren against Somerset at Taunton on 15-16 July 1895. Opening the innings, he was seventh out at 792 after giving only two chances – the first when he was 262 and batting for 470 minutes. MacLaren hit a six, 62 fours, 11 threes, 37 twos and 63 singles. His score passed the previous highest of 344 by W.G. Grace and remained the world first-class record until Bill Ponsford scored 429 in 479 minutes in February 1923.

HIGHEST TEAM SCORE

Lancashire's highest score is 863 against Surrey at The Oval in May 1990. Neil Fairbrother scored 366 and with Mike Atherton scoring 191, the two batsmen added 364 runs for the third wicket. Lancashire fell just 24 runs short of the record score of 887 in the County Championship. Surrey made the highest score against Lancashire, declaring their first innings on 707 for nine in the same match.

HILTON, MALCOLM

Starting his career as a fast bowler with Werneth in the Central Lancashire League, Malcolm Hilton made his name as a left-arm spinner and in only his third first-class game for Lancashire dismissed Don Bradman twice in the county's game against the Austra-

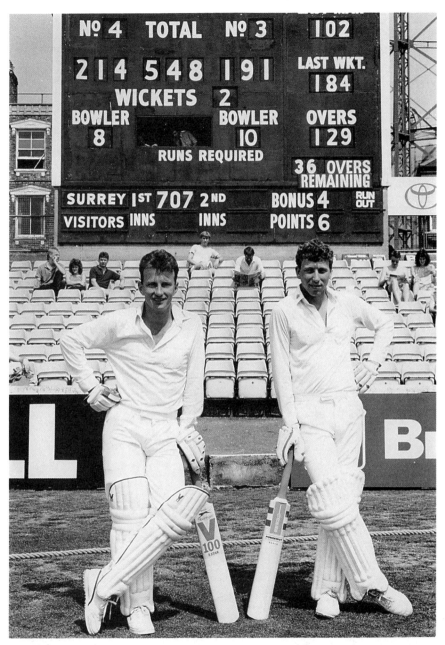

Neil Fairbrother and Mike Atherton in front of the Oval scoreboard after adding a record 364 for the third wicket against Surrey in 1990.

lians at Old Trafford. However, it was 1950 before he gained a regular place in the Lancashire side and by the end of the season, he had taken 127 wickets at 15.32 runs apiece. It was also the summer in which he made the first of his four Test appearances in which he took fifteen wickets at 33.64 runs each.

His best season for Lancashire was 1956 when he took 150 wickets and was chosen as one of Wisden's Cricketers of the Year. His best figures that summer were eight for 39 against Somerset at Weston-super-Mare. A flamboyant batsman, his only hundred came in 1955, batting at Number 9 in the match against Northamptonshire. He played his last game for the county in 1961 when still only 33 after taking 926 wickets for Lancashire at an average of 18.81 runs each.

HONOURS

County Champions   1881, 1897, 1904, 1926, 1927, 1928, 1930, 1934
Joint Champions   1879, 1882, 1889, 1950
Nat West/Gillette Cup Winners   1970, 1971, 1972, 1975, 1990, 1996
Benson and Hedges Cup Winners   1984, 1990, 1995, 1996
John Player/Refuge Assurance League Champions   1969, 1970, 1989
Refuge Assurance Cup Winners   1988

1988 Refuge Assurance Cup Final Winners

HOPWOOD, LEN

CHURCHMAN'S CIGARETTES

J. L. HOPWOOD

Len Hopwood joined the Old Trafford staff in 1922 and made his first team debut the following season, but in those days, the money was not that good and in 1925 he left the club to go and play with Wallasey. He returned to the county in 1928, helping them win the County Championship for the third year in succession.

An important member of the Lancashire side that won the County Championship again in 1930 and 1934, he missed scoring 1,000 runs in a season only once in the ten years leading up to the outbreak of the Second World War.

The 1933 season was his best as a batsman, as he scored 1,972 runs at 46.95. In 1934 he achieved the 'double' with 1,672 runs and 111 wickets, scoring a career best 220 in the match against Gloucestershire at Bristol. He performed the 'double' again in 1935 with 1,538 runs and 103 wickets.

Hopwood played in two Tests for England in 1934 but failed to do himself justice and was not selected again. Playing in 397 games for Lancashire, he scored 15,519 runs at 30.01 and took 672 wickets at 22.18 runs apiece. The Newton Hyde-born all-rounder had the distinction of becoming the first former professional cricketer to be appointed President of Lancashire when he took up office in 1981.

HORNBY, ALBERT HENRY

The son of Albert Neilson 'Monkey' Hornby he first appeared for the county in 1899 and during that summer the two of them appeared for the county for the only time in the match against Leicestershire.

Though the young Hornby didn't emulate his father by playing at Test level, he matched everything he had done while playing for Lancashire. After his debut season, he missed the next three years and it was 1904 before he made the first of his eight centuries for Lancashire.

The following season, Hornby played what was easily his most spectacular innings, hitting a century against Somerset in just 43 minutes. It remained the fastest for the county until Steve O'Shaughnessy took advantage of some poor Leicestershire bowling in 1983.

Hornby usually batted in Lancashire's lower middle order but in 1907 he opened the innings with MacLaren and scored 125 at almost a run a minute as the two batsmen put on 182 for the first wicket. His highest score for the county came in 1912 when he hit 129 against Surrey at the Oval. That season, Hornby and Jack Sharp added 245 for the seventh wicket in the match against Leicestershire at Old Trafford, a partnership which is still the county record for that wicket.

COUNTY CRICKETERS.

MR. A. H. HORNBY.
LANCASHIRE.

HORNBY, ALBERT NEILSON

Involved with the county as a player and president for over fifty years, Albert Neilson 'Monkey' Hornby first came to attention of cricketing circles when he played for Harrow at Lord's. His father who was a Member of Parliament, hoped his son would go on to Oxford University to complete his education but the young Hornby had other ideas and in 1867, the Blackburn-born batsman played his first game for Lancashire. He scored the first of his seventeen centuries for Lancashire in 1870 when he made 132 against Hampshire at Southampton.

When Edmund Rowley resigned the captaincy in 1880, Hornby was asked to replace him. A man of immense strength, he was certainly well equipped for leadership. An all-round sportsman, he played soccer for Blackburn Rovers and appeared in nine international matches for England's Rugby Union side as well as excelling at athletics and boxing.

Hornby captained Lancashire from 1880 to 1891 and then shared the captaincy over the next two seasons with Sydney Crosfield, even though he had told the Committee he would be unable to turn out on a regular basis. Archie MacLaren captained the side for the next three seasons but in 1897, Hornby was again persuaded to take charge of the county side.

He played the last of his 292 games for Lancashire in 1899 when he was 52 years of age, scoring 53 in his last innings. When his playing days were finished, Hornby became Lancashire's president, a position he held from 1894 to 1916.

HOWARD, NIGEL

Educated at Rossall School and later Manchester University, Nigel Howard made his Lancashire debut in 1946, though it was another two years before he scored his maiden first-class century, 145 against Derbyshire at Old Trafford.

He was appointed captain of Lancashire in 1949 and was the youngest ever captain of the county. In 1950 he helped the bring the title of joint champions to Old Trafford as Lancashire shared the championship title with Surrey. That season, Howard scored 1,174 runs at an average of 37.97.

In 1951, he captained the Gentlemen v Players at Lord's and in 1951-52, he played four times for England during the tour of India, captaining a side that contained other Lancashire players in Hilton, Statham and Tattersall.

Lancashire ended the 1953 season in third place but at the age of just 28, Nigel Howard felt he could no longer devote enough time to the game and retired to concentrate on his business interests.

HUGHES, DAVID

The son of a Bolton League professional, David Hughes began his cricketing career with his home town team of Newton-le-Willows before playing for Farnworth in the Bolton League. He joined Lancashire in 1967 but it was in the summer of 1971 that Hughes first made his mark.

His remarkable match winning innings of 26 not out against Gloucestershire in the semi-final of the Gillette Cup transformed the popular all-rounder into a Lancastrian folk hero.

As a bowler in Jack Bond's side, Hughes was given plenty opportunity to turn his arm over and in 1970 and 1971 he took 82 wickets in each season. During the five seasons in which Bond was in charge,

David Hughes

Hughes took 296 wickets but when Bond departed, Hughes was left to concentrate solely on his batting.

In the Gillette Cup Final of 1976, he hit Indian Test bowler Bishen Bedi for 26 off the last over in Lancashire's innings but unfortunately it failed to bring victory to the Red-Rose side.

In 1981, he passed the 1,000 run mark for the first time and scored his first Championship century, 126 against Warwickshire at Old Trafford. By 1986, Hughes was leading the Lancashire 2nd XI to the Championship and the following season was reinstated to the county first team as captain. In his first season in charge, he was chosen as one of Wisden's Five Cricketers of the Year and voted as Captain of the Year by The Cricket Writers Club as he almost led the county to their first outright County Championship since 1934.

Hughes led Lancashire to the first ever Refuge Assurance Cup Final where they beat Worcestershire and in 1989 the county won the Sunday League title for the first time in nineteen years.

In 1990, Lancashire won both the Benson and Hedge Cup and the Nat West Trophy. One of the best all-rounders to captain the county, he played his last game in 1991 after scoring 10,126 runs at 22.01 and taking 637 wickets at 29.78 runs each.

HUNDRED WICKETS IN A SEASON

Twenty-nine Lancashire players have performed the feat of taking 100 wickets or more for the county in a season with Johnny Briggs having done so on 11 occasions. He was also the first player to achieve the feat in 1887 when he took 102 wickets at 16.90 runs each; he was closely followed that season by Alec Watson who took 100 wickets at 14.82 runs apiece. The last player to take a hundred wickets for the county was Peter Lee in 1975 when he took 112 wickets at 18.45 runs each.

IDDISON, ROGER

A Yorkshireman born in Bedale, Roger Iddison was one of the finest professional cricketers of his day. He first played for Lancashire in 1865 and the following year scored the county's first century, 106 out of their total of 321 for eight against Surrey at the Oval.

He went on the first tour of Australia in 1861-62 and played in All-England and other representative games. He played for Lancashire up until 1870 but only appeared in sixteen matches, scoring 621 runs and taking 56 wickets.

He captained Yorkshire from 1863 to 1870 and though he played for both Lancashire and Yorkshire in the same season, whenever the two counties played each other, he always opted for the county of his birth.

IDDON, JACK

The son of a professional cricketer, Jack Iddon played his early cricket with Neston and Leyland Motors before making his Lancashire debut in 1924. It was another two years before he was a regular in the county side but 1928 before he began to show his true capabilities with both the bat and the ball. In that summer of 1928, he scored 1,353 runs at an average of 52.03 and took 63 wickets at a cost of 25 runs apiece. He then proceeded to score 1,000 runs in each of the next twelve seasons with a best of 2,381 runs in 1934.

It was this form that earned him a place in the MCC team to tour the West Indies, where he played in four Tests. He played another against South Africa at Trent Bridge in 1935 ending his international career with two half-centuries.

In the Roses match of 1934, he scored a quite superb 142 not out when the Yorkshire bowlers were on top and in 1937 produced match winning bowling figures of nine for 42 at Bramall Lane on a wearing wicket. When the Second World War was over, Iddon who had scored 21,975 runs and taken 533 wickets for Lancashire decided to play for the county as an amateur, but tragically the man who might have even captained the county side, was killed in a motor accident.

IKIN, JACK

Jack Ikin was only 16 years of age when he played for his native county Staffordshire in the Minor Counties Championship before making his Lancashire debut in 1939. When the war was over, he soon established himself in the Lancashire team and actually played for England in the first post-war Test against India before he had been capped by his county.

He toured Australia and New Zealand in 1946-47 with the MCC team and was a member of Gubby Allen's side to the West Indies in 1947-48. His other tour was to India in 1950-51 where he headed the batting averages in the unofficial Tests with 625 runs at an average of 89.28. He played the last of his eighteen Tests for England in 1955, nine years after he had made his debut.

For Lancashire, he played in 288 matches, scoring 14,327 runs at 37.70 and taking 278 wickets at 28.79 runs each. He scored 23 centuries for the county with a highest of 192 against Oxford University in 1951. His best piece of bowling for the county was six for 21 against Nottinghamshire at Old Trafford in 1947 whilst in 1949 he performed the hat-trick against Somerset at Taunton.

After leaving Lancashire in 1957 he returned to captain Staffordshire in Minor Counties cricket before ending his playing days in 1968.

INDIA

In 1911, India sent her first representative side to England, when a side captained by H.H. the Maharajah of Patiala played fourteen matches. Lancashire defeated the tourists at Old Trafford with India being bowled out for 85, their lowest ever total against the Red-Rose county.

At Aigburth in 1932, a rain-ruined match was enlivened by an entertaining innings of 131 not out from Number 10 batsman Amar Singh, as India totalled 493, still their highest score against Lancashire.

Though India were humiliated during the summer of 1952 by England and in the Old Trafford Test were bowled out for 58 and 82 to lose by an innings and 207 runs, they did dismiss Lancashire for 68 in their match against the Red-Rose side. In 1961, Ken Grieves hit 202 against India at Blackpool to record the highest individual score by a Lancashire player in this fixture.

Lancashire's highest score against the Indian tourists came in 1974 at Old Trafford, when they scored 511. Lancashire's record of first-class matches v India is:

P.	W.	L.	D.	Tied
13	2	3	8	0

INJURIES

One of the most unusual injuries to occur on a cricket field befell Lancashire's Frank Hayes, who fractured a leg while taking a run in a match at Lord's in 1982.

K

KENT

Founded in 1859, Kent have won the County Championship on six occasions, four times in the 'Golden Age' of cricket – 1906, 1909, 1910 and 1913 and twice more recently – 1970 and 1978. A consistently successful one day side, they have won nine trophies: four Sunday Leagues (1972, 1973, 1976 and 1995) three Benson and Hedges Cups (1973, 1976 and 1978) and two Gillette Cups (1967 and 1974).

When Lancashire met Kent in 1883, Lord Harris made a sparkling 118 out of Kent's first innings total of 309. Crossland took six of the last seven wickets to fall after Kent had been 280 for three. Lancashire were dismissed for 206 and were forced to follow on, but with Hornby following up his first innings score of 88 with 96 in the second, they scored 238. Needing 136 to win, Kent were bowled out for 65 with Barlow taking six for 32 in Lancashire's famous victory.

Freak weather conditions delayed and then spoiled the opening day of the 1886 meeting at Old Trafford. Dense fog held up play for 45 minutes, then gale force winds blew lots of hats from the heads of spectators all across the field!

When the two sides met at Tonbridge in 1892, Lancashire had scored 484 and Kent were 47 for two when rain stopped play for two and a half hours. Mold and Briggs then took 16 wickets in 85 minutes so that at the close of play, Kent still needed 345 to avoid an innings defeat with just two wickets in hand. Frank Marchant, the Kent captain refused to continue and so play had to start early the following day in order for Lancashire to catch the 3.00pm. train from St Pancras. Arthur Mold took nine for 29 in Kent's second innings – the best return of his career.

When the counties met in 1930, Kent were top and Lancashire in second place, eleven points adrift. Ted McDonald took eleven wickets and Richard Tyldesley seven, in an innings win for Lancashire. Bill Farrimond deputising for George Duckworth scored 46 not out and had seven victims in an innings, with six catches all off the bowling of McDonald.

In 1935, Kent's captain Percy Chapman set Lancashire a victory target of 396 in five hours in the match at Dover. Watson and Hopwood put on 103 for the first wicket and then Hopwood and Iddon added 149 for the second. When Iddon was out at 327, he had scored 141 in two and a half hours. The Red-Rose county won by five wickets with 18 minutes remaining.

Despite Aravinda de Silva's magnificent innings of 112 in the 1995 Benson and Hedges Cup Final, Lancashire won by 35 runs to win the trophy for a third time. Lancashire's record of first-class matches v Kent is:

P.	W.	L.	D.	Tied
200	82	48	70	0

KENYON, MYLES

Appointed Lancashire captain in 1919, the Bury-born Kenyon inherited players such as Harry Dean, Harry Makepeace, Cec Parkin, Jack

Sharp and J.T. and Ernest Tyldesley. In his first season, he led the team to fifth place in the County Championship whilst in 1920, he broke down midway through the season, handing over the reins to Jack Sharp. The county finished fifth in each of the next two seasons before Kenyon officially retired. He did play a couple of games in 1923 and 1924 but he never had any great pretensions about his playing ability, never bowling and only scoring 1,435 runs at an average of 14.79 in the 91 matches in which he played.

He certainly helped lay the foundations for the county's success that was just round the corner. In fact, he was so highly thought of, that he was elected Club President in 1936 and 1937.

LANCASTER

After some important local matches were played at the ground – Eighteen of the District (1891) Eighteen of North Lancashire and District (1902) and Eighteen of the District (1904) all v Lancashire County XII – yet was decided in 1914 to allocate a County Championship match to be played at Lancaster. Lancashire's opponents were Warwickshire, who defeated the Red-Rose county by 173 runs. That same weekend, war with Germany commenced and first-class cricket never re-appeared at Lancaster.

LEE, PETER

Signed from Northamptonshire as support to Lever and Shuttleworth, Peter Lee was so successful that he soon became Lancashire's number one bowler. In 1973 he became the first Lancashire bowler to reach one hundred wickets since Ken Higgs in 1968. His 101 wickets, 144 in all competitions made him the leading wicket-taker in the championship.

In 1975, he took 112 championship wickets at 18.45 runs each, a superb achievement with a best of seven for 8 against Warwickshire at Edgbaston. The following season he took 66 wickets, the only Lancashire bowler to exceed fifty wickets.

Peter Lee continued to play for the county until 1982, finishing his career with 496 wickets at 23.82 runs each and a best of eight for 34 against Sussex at Hove in 1973.

LEICESTERSHIRE

Founded in 1879, Leicestershire for many years a 'Cinderella' county, became a power to be reckoned with after the appointment of Ray Illingworth as captain in 1969. The county were the inaugural winners of the Benson and Hedges Cup in 1972 and also won it in 1975 and 1985; they won the Sunday League in 1974 and 1977 and captured the County Championship title in 1975 and 1996 when they lost only one game.

In 1906, Leicestershire were the first visitors to play at Blackpool in a Championship match. Lancashire won by an innings and 41 runs with Jack Sharp scoring 111 and Bill Gregson, a fast bowler from Lancaster taking five for 8 including a hat-trick.

When Lancashire played Leicestershire at Old Trafford in 1924, Dick Tyldesley wasn't introduced into the attack until the visitors were 78 for three but in five overs he took five wickets without conceding a run and they were all out for 89 with seven of their batsmen failing to score. His fourth wicket was his 100th of the season and it was only 3 July. Cec Parkin wasn't to be outdone, for in Leicestershire's second innings he took the first seven wickets to fall before rain forced the players to leave the field. Lancashire claimed their ninth wicket on the stroke of lunch but Alec Skelding the last man was already on his way to the wicket and Major Fowke the Leicestershire captain sportingly insisted that play continue. Twenty-five minutes later Tyldesley captured the last wicket and as the players left the field, the heavens opened and the ground was flooded!

Lancashire created an unusual record in the 1956 match against Leicestershire at Old Trafford when they won without losing a wicket. After no play on the first day, Leicestershire were bowled out for 108. Dyson and Wharton then scored 166 without trouble and Edrich declared first thing the next morning. Lancashire then bowled Leicestershire out for 122 and knocked off the 65 runs needed for victory without loss.

Leicestershire were Lancashire's opponents in the first ever Gillette Cup match. Peter Marner, who later went on to play for Leicestershire scored 121 in Lancashire's total of 304 for nine. Maurice Hallam scored 106 but Lancashire won by 101 runs.

In the last game of the 1983 season, Steve O'Shaughnessy equalled Percy Fender's 63 year old world record for the fastest century in the match against Leicestershire. Roger Tolchard soon had his spinners operating and after they had taken four bowling points in dismissing Lancashire for 236 they needed one for batting to finish fourth in the Championship. Once this had been won, they declared 86 behind, whereupon Gower and Whitaker fed the Lancashire batsmen with long hops and full tosses. Fowler and O'Shaughnessy added 201 in 43 minutes, the fastest first-class double-century partnership. O'Shaughnessy's century in 35 minutes included five 6s and seventeen 4s.

Lancashire's record of first-class matches v Leicestershire is:

P.	W.	L.	D.	Tied
146	72	18	56	0

LEVER, PETER

Peter Lever

First appearing for Lancashire in 1960, he had to serve long and hard in the shadows of the county's international bowlers, Statham and Higgs and was not capped until 1965.

In his early years with the county, he batted well enough to hold down a middle-order place and in 1963 and 1966, scored over 500 runs in each season as well as taking more than 50 wickets.

In 1970, when almost 30, Lever played for England against the Rest of the World side. In the last game of the series he produced what were then, the best figures of his career – seven for 83, taking the wickets of Barlow, Pollock, Muhtaq, Sobers, Lloyd, Procter and Intikhab. In the winter of 1970-71 he toured Australia and played in five Tests, making significant contributions to England regaining the Ashes. He toured Down Under again in 1974-75 and in the last Test at Melbourne took six for 38. In 1971, he scored 88 not out against India in the Old Trafford Test, his only half-century in seventeen Test matches in which he captured 41 wickets at 36.80 runs apiece.

For Lancashire he took 716 first-class wickets at 26.64 runs each and was a vital member of the county's side in the early 1970s, when in 167 limited-over matches he took 256 wickets at 17.53 runs each.

LISTER, LIONEL

In only his second match for Lancashire in 1933, Lionel Lister scored 100 not out against Middlesex at Old Trafford and followed it up in his next two games with 96 against Worcestershire and 95 against Leicestershire.

By the following season, he had established himself in the Lancashire middle-order and when Peter Eckersley left at the end of the 1935 season, Lister was appointed captain. His four years in charge were poor ones and though he hit an unbeaten 104 against Middlesex, the county dropped to eleventh place in 1936.

By the end of May 1938, Lancashire were in first place in the Championship as Lister led them to six wins out of the first seven matches but after a disastrous defeat in the Roses game, they fell away and had to be content with fourth place.

In 1939 he missed a number of matches due to his Territorial Army duties and when cricket resumed after the hostilities his business commitments prevented him from playing. The county continued to recognise his abilities, electing him President in 1969.

LLOYD, CLIVE

Born in Georgetown, Guyana, Clive Lloyd was arguably Lancashire's greatest-ever batsman. He arrived in England in 1967 to play as professional for Haslingden and when his contract expired he joined Lancashire. Though he failed to score a century in 1969, he helped the county win the new John Player Sunday League. His first century

Clive Lloyd

arrived in 1970 in the match against Kent at Dartford, hitting 163 in 145 minutes, including seven 6's. Also that summer he scored an unbeaten 134 against Somerset in the Sunday League, still Lancashire's highest individual score in that competition.

The West Indian took a particular liking to Warwickshire, making his highest score for the county, 217 not out against them at Old Trafford in 1971. Warwickshire were Lancashire's opponents in the 1972 Gillette Cup Final where Lloyd blasted a magnificent match winning innings of 126.

In 1974, Lloyd was appointed captain of the West Indies, a position he was to hold for eleven years. He appeared in 110 Tests, scoring 7,515 runs at 46.67 and a highest score of 242 not out against India at Bombay in his first series as captain.

In 1975, he hit six centuries for Lancashire, four of them in successive matches and led the West Indies to victory in the Prudential World Cup, scoring 102 off 82 balls against Australia in the final.

In 1980 when Gillette ended their sponsorship, Clive Lloyd was awarded the 'Man of the Series' trophy as the player who had made the greatest contribution to the competition. The following year he was elected captain of Lancashire, but unfortunately during his three years in charge and a further year in 1986, Lloyd couldn't produce a winning formula for the Red-Rose county that he had for the West Indies.

In first-class matches for Lancashire, he scored 12,764 runs at an average of 44.94, the second highest behind Ernest Tyldesley of a Lancashire player.

LLOYD, DAVID

When David Lloyd first appeared at Old Trafford, he was regarded as a highly promising left-arm spinner with the possibility of his batting being an added bonus.

When Jack Bond was appointed captain in 1968, he promoted Lloyd to open the innings with Barry Wood it what proved to be a very effective move, though he did take seven for 38 against Gloucestershire at Lydney in his early years.

During the summer of 1972, Lloyd hit six centuries and with Wood, shared in a first wicket stand of 299 against Leicestershire. In 1973, Lloyd replaced Bond as captain and was chosen to lead Young

David Lloyd

England against a West Indies side that contained Clive Lloyd. The following season, David Lloyd was chosen to play in the first of what was to be nine Tests for England. After scoring 46 at Lord's, he hit a magnificent 214 not out against India at Edgbaston. Also in that 1974 season, Lloyd captained the county unbeaten through the County Championship though they only finished in eighth position.

In 1975, he led Lancashire to victory over Middlesex in the Gillette Cup Final but at the end of the 1977 season decided to stand down as captain. He continued to play for the county until 1983, ending his playing career with 17,877 runs at 33.41 and 234 wickets at 29.94 runs each.

Affectionately known as 'Bumble' he joined the first-class umpires list, played for Cumberland and was Development Officer for Kwik Cricket before joining Lancashire as coach in 1992. He is currently occupied in a similar capacity for England.

LOWEST

Lancashire's lowest score is 25 made against Derbyshire on 26 May 1871 at Old Trafford – it was the first important match ever played by the visitors.

Glamorgan made the lowest score against Lancashire, being all out for 22 on the Aigburth Ground, Liverpool on 15 May 1924. The wicket was so difficult that in two hours twenty minutes, both sides were in and out, Lancashire making 49. The county's best bowling figures in that match were by Cecil Parkin whose analysis was:

O.	M.	R.	W.
8	5	6	6

LYTHAM

Lancashire made their first visit to Church Road, Lytham for a Championship match in 1985 when Northamptonshire were the opponents, but unfortunately it was rain affected.

The club had staged benefit matches for Lancashire players with crowds of around 3,000 but in 1986 when Glamorgan visited Lytham, 3,500 saw John Abrahams almost become the first player to hit a first-class century at the ground. That honour fell to Essex's John

Stephenson in 1989, a match in which Lancashire's Graham Lloyd scored 100 in the visitors seven wicket victory.

In 1992, John Crawley scored a masterly 172 runs from 345 balls with 18 fours as Lancashire won by 86 runs with just 13 balls remaining.

McDONALD, TED

After just one year as an international fast bowler, Ted McDonald retired from the Australian team, having taken 43 wickets in his 11 Tests. He first played for Lancashire in 1924 after a spell as professional for Nelson in the Lancashire League but he wasn't fully available and with the summer being a very wet one, he failed to achieve his maximum effectiveness. However, he more than made up for this in 1925, when he took 182 wickets in Championship games, 205 in all matches at slightly over 18 runs apiece. He performed the hat-trick against Sussex at Hove and repeated the achievement against Kent at Dover the following season. That season of 1926 saw him hit his only century in a Championship fixture, when he hit a quick-fire unbeaten 100 against Middlesex at Old Trafford.

His best season for the county was 1928 when at the age of 36, he took 178 wickets in the Championship, 190 in all matches at 19 runs apiece. In the space of two weeks, he took 35 wickets for 526 runs, including fifteen for 154 in the match against Kent at Old Trafford.

In 1930, he took the third hat-trick of his career at Edgbaston and later that season to his own delight he took the wicket of Australia's premier batsman, Don Bradman. Having been unable to produce his old pace in the summer of 1931, his contract was terminated a year earlier than agreed by mutual consent. The popular Australian finished with 1,053 wickets at 20.96 runs apiece.

He had played in a benefit match in Manchester and was returning home to the Raikes Park Hotel he managed in Blackpool, when his car was in a collision with another. He was unhurt but walking back along the road to offer help to the other driver, he was hit by another vehicle and killed.

MCINTYRE, BILL

Nottinghamshire-born Bill McIntyre played for his native county from 1869 to 1871 before joining Lancashire and playing for them from 1872 to 1880. One of the best bowlers in the country, he headed national averages on three occasions during his career with Lancashire. In his first season at Old Trafford, he took 41 wickets at 5.65 runs each and the following summer, 63 wickets at 8.38 runs each. He topped the national averages for a third and final time in 1876 when he took 89 wickets at 11.41 runs each.

His best figures were eight for 31 against Derbyshire at Derby in 1877 when he had match figures of fifteen for 47. Playing his last game for the county in 1880, he took 441 wickets at 1.65 runs apiece.

MACLAREN, ARCHIE

Captain of Lancashire from 1894 to 1896 and again from 1900 to 1907, Archie MacLaren made his county debut against Sussex at Hove in 1890, scoring 108 in 130 minutes.

In 1895, his second year of captaincy, MacLaren led the Red-Rose county to runners-up in the County Championship and in the match against Somerset at Taunton achieved a personal distinction. He scored 424 runs in an innings that lasted ten minutes under eight hours. The following year he scored 226 not out against Kent at Canterbury as Lancashire again ended the season as runners-up.

During his second spell as captain, he led Lancashire to the Championship in 1904, the county going through the season undefeated.

MacLaren played in 35 Tests for England between 1894 an 1909, scoring 1,931 runs at an average of 33.87 with five centuries. His first came during the 1894-95 tour of Australia at Melbourne in the fifth Test, when his innings of 120 helped England to clinch the series 3-2.

Three years later, when A.E. Stoddart took another side Down Under, MacLaren hit centuries at Sydney and Adelaide. His last century innings against the Australians came at Trent Bridge in 1905 when he made a masterly 140 in England's second innings. MacLaren also captained England in 22 matches, though his captaincy was at times open to criticism.

Archie MacLaren

For Lancashire, he scored 15,735 runs at an average of 33.34, a great achievement when one considers that the wickets in those days were of variable quality and more often than not were quite unplayable.

Following his retirement from the first-class game, MacLaren at the age of 51, played for MCC against New Zealand at Wellington in 1923 and scored 200 not out. He was also county coach but after a number of disagreements with the Lancashire Committee, he ended his long association with the county.

MAKEPEACE, HARRY

Though he made his debut for Lancashire in 1906, Harry Makepeace had to wait until 1911 before he scored his first century for the county, 139 against Worcestershire at Stourbridge. He was desperately unlucky in 1907 when during the match against Sussex at Eastbourne, MacLaren declared at lunch with Makepeace 99 not out. When MacLaren at looked at the scoreboard, Makepeace's score read 100 but it was later discovered that the scorer had made a mistake, Makepeace was a run short!

In 1911, he scored 1,000 runs for the first time, the first of twelve successive seasons in which he passed that landmark. His best season for the county was 1926 when he scored 2,340 runs at an average of 48.75.

Makepeace played in four Tests for England, scoring 117 and 54 in the fourth Test of the 1920-21 tour at Melbourne. He was also a soccer international, making four appearances for England and playing in two successive FA Cup Finals for Everton in 1906 and 1907.

Towards the end of his playing career, he was appointed assistant coach at Old Trafford and

COUNTY CRICKETERS.

H. MAKEPEACE, LANCASHIRE.

when he eventually did retire at the age of 49, he had scored 25,207 runs at an average of 36.37. He subsequently became Chief Coach at Lancashire, a position he held until well after the Second World War.

MARNER, PETER

Playing in the match against Sussex at Hove in 1952, Peter Marner at 16 years 150 days became Lancashire's youngest ever debutant. Marner was a powerful hitter of the ball and the following season when still only 17 hit four 6's and a four in a half-hour stay at the wicket against Somerset at Bath which brought him 44 runs and Lancashire victory inside a day.

In 1960, he scored 44 against Nottinghamshire at Southport, all in boundary strokes – a record – with four 6's and five 4's. Again at Southport in 1962, he hit five 6's and fifteen 4's in an unbeaten 106 against Warwickshire.

In 1963 in the first ever Gillette Cup match, he scored 121 against Leicestershire to become the scorer of the first century in a major inter-county limited overs competition. However, at the end of the following season, Marner was sacked. He had scored 10,312 runs for Lancashire at 29.21 with ten centuries. The pick of these was 142 not out against Leicestershire, the county he played for from 1965 to 1970.

MIDDLESEX

Founded in 1863, Middlesex won the unofficial county title in 1866 and won ten official Championships, with their last being in 1993. Middlesex have also won seven one-day competitions; the Gillette Cup in 1977 and 1980, the Benson and Hedges Cup in 1983 and 1986, the Nat West trophy in 1984 and 1988 and the Sunday League in 1992.

Middlesex were Lancashire's opponents in their first true county game in 1865. The first innings scores were tied, though in Lancashire's second innings, Middlesex's Vyell Edward Walker took all ten wickets. However, Lancashire won by 62 runs as Reynolds and Iddison bowled well.

When Lancashire played Middlesex at Lord's in 1937, 'Big Jim' Smith lost the ball by hitting it over the grandstand and according to Bill Edrich 'twice as high as the statue of Father Time'.

The two counties also met in the 1975 Gillette Cup Final with Lancashire winning by seven wickets thanks to Clive Lloyd's unbeaten 73.Lancashire's record of first-class matches v Middlesex is:

P.	W.	L.	D.	Tied
178	52	52	74	0

MOLD, ARTHUR

Born in the Northamptonshire village of Middleton Cheney, he qualified by residence to play for Lancashire and made his debut for the Red-Rose county in 1889.

In his first season he took 102 wickets at 11.83 runs each and finished third in the national averages. One of the fastest bowlers in the country, he took thirteen for 111 in the Roses match at Huddersfield. He certainly enjoyed playing against Yorkshire, for in 1890 he took nine for 40 at Old Trafford and thirteen for 74 at Huddersfield.

Though there were concerns about Mold's action in his early days, the suspicions of 'throwing' had not developed as they were to by the turn of the century. W.G. Grace had no doubts about Mold's action and dubbed him 'the fairest of fast bowlers'.

In 1891, Mold took 129 wickets at 12.62 runs each and the following year was chosen as one of Wisden's Five Cricketers of the Year, as he once again took over a hundred wicket, including a career best nine for 29 against Kent at Tonbridge.

In 1893, he took 142 wickets for Lancashire and was chosen to play in three Test matches against Australia, though sadly he failed to do himself justice.

The following two seasons were Mold's most successful. In all matches in each season he took over 200 wickets. In 1894 in the match against Somerset, he took seven for 10 including a hat-trick and ten balls later, three wickets in four balls. In 1895 he took four wickets in four balls against Nottinghamshire, ending the summer in which W.G. Grace scored a thousand runs in May by taking 182 Championship wickets.

He was then plagued by injuries, though in 1899 he took 115 wickets at just over 18 runs each. In 1901 he fell foul of umpire Jim Phillips who repeatedly no-balled him and though Mold's contemporaries thought his action fair, the damage had been done and a career in which he took 1,541 wickets at 15.15 runs apiece was at an end.

MOST RUNS

The following batsmen have scored the most runs for Lancashire.

		Runs	Average
1.	Ernest Tyldesley	34,222	45.20
2.	Johnny Tyldesley	31,949	41.38
3.	Cyril Washbrook	27,863	42.15
4.	Harry Makepeace	25,207	36.37
5.	Frank Watson	22,833	37.06
6.	Jack Sharp	22,015	31.18
7.	Jack Iddon	21,975	37.05
8.	Ken Grieves	20,802	33.39
9.	Charlie Hallows	20,142	39.72
10.	Alan Wharton	17,921	33.55

MOST WICKETS

The following bowlers have taken the most wickets for Lancashire.

		Wickets	Average
1.	Brian Statham	1,816	15.12
2.	Johnny Briggs	1,696	15.60
3.	Arthur Mold	1,543	15.15
4.	Richard Tyldesley	1,449	16.65
5.	Alec Watson	1,308	13.39
6.	Harry Dean	1,267	18.01
7.	Roy Tattersall	1,168	17.39
8.	Ted McDonald	1,053	20.96
9.	Ken Higgs	1,033	22.90
10.	Dick Pollard	1,015	22.15

MUSEUM

The rebuilding operations at Old Trafford in 1982 incorporated a purpose-built museum, which was completed in the autumn of 1983. All members and visitors are welcome and there is free entrance on match days to see the great array of cricket memorabilia.

There are match balls from the 1850s, old paintings and scorecards along with the scorebook recording Archie MacLaren's record innings of 424 against Somerset. Early photographs from the formation of the county club have been preserved along with autographs, menu cards and newspapers.

There are also scrapbooks, bats and plates relating to the Tyldesley's, Walter Brearley, Sydney Barnes and Ted McDonald. Autographed bats from county and international teams blend in with handkerchiefs, one of which was presented to Eddie Paynter for his epic four-hour Ashes-winning innings at Brisbane in 1933. Old Trafford also has one of the best libraries on the county circuit, under the watchful eye of the Rev Malcolm Lorimer.

MUSICAL TALENTS

Dick Pollard, who took 1,015 wickets for Lancashire at 22.15 each was an accomplished pianist, whilst wicket-keeper Frank Parr, who played in 48 matches in the 1950s, played trombone in a traditional jazz group. In recent years, Graeme Fowler, the Lancashire and England opening batsman, was an accomplished drummer.

NAT WEST TROPHY

The Nat West Bank took over the sponsorship from Gillette in 1981 but though Lancashire reached the final in 1989, they had to wait a further year for their first success. Lancashire have won the Nat West Trophy on two occasions:

| 1990 | Northamptonshire 171 | Lancashire 173 for 3 |
| 1996 | Lancashire 186 | Essex 57 |

In the 1996 final, Glen Chapple took six for 18 to give Lancashire a 129 run victory. Other Nat West records include:

Highest Innings Total	372 for five v Gloucestershire at Old Trafford in 1990
Lowest Completed Innings Total	105 v Middlesex at Lord's in 1984
Highest Individual Score	122 by G. Fowler v Gloucestershire at Bristol in 1984
Best Bowling Performance	5 for 13 by P. de Freitas v Cumberland at Kendal in 1989
Highest Partnership	167 for 1st wicket by M. Atherton and S. Titchard v Worcestershire at Old Trafford in 1995.

NELSON

Australian fast bowler Ted McDonald was engaged as professional by Nelson and in 1923 took 112 wickets, including all ten for 18 runs against Burnley. Lancashire were eager to sign him and in order for Nelson to agree his release, Lancashire played two county games at Nelson in 1925 and 1926.

Derbyshire were the first visitors to the ground and were beaten by 97 runs with McDonald on his 'home ground' taking four for 47. The following year Essex provided the opposition and Ernest Tyldesley scored a century in a drawn match. Because of the success of these fixtures, the county allocated further matches for the next three seasons. Charlie Hallows scored centuries in victories over Warwickshire in 1928 and 1929, whilst McDonald destroyed Leicestershire in 1930. When the fixtures were switched to midweek, they were not as popular with the spectators.

The last county match at Nelson was in 1938 when Somerset were the visitors. The match however, was something of a disaster with only two and three-quarter hours of play possible in three days, although Lancashire were dismissed for 79, their lowest total of the season. Lancashire remained undefeated at Nelson, winning five out of nine matches.

NEW YEAR'S CARD

After receiving their Christmas card from Lancashire, the Nottinghamshire C.C.C. naturally replied with a New Year's card to Old Trafford. It read:

Lancashire County Cricket Club

The only rules necessary for players in the County Eleven are that they shall neither have been born in, nor reside in, Lancashire. Sutton-in-Ashfield men (Briggs and Crossland) will have the preference.

NEW ZEALAND

New Zealand first visited these shores for a Test series against England in 1931. It was during that summer in the match at Aigburth, that both sides recorded their highest score in these matches. Lancashire scored 487 and New Zealand 410 for nine in a drawn encounter. New Zealand's lowest score against Lancashire is 104 and came in the Old Trafford match of 1965, whilst Lancashire's lowest score in these fixtures is 116 and came in 1973. Lancashire's record of first-class matches v New Zealand is:

P.	W.	L.	D.	Tied
12	3	2	7	0

NICKNAMES

Many players in the club's history have been fondly known by their nickname.

¤ 'Th'owd chain horse' was a title not bestowed lightly on Dick Pollard. They don't complain and neither did he – a great hearted fast-medium bowler, he would toil endlessly through the heat and burden of the day.

¤ 'The Whippet' was the somewhat fanciful nickname given to Brian Statham, though he preferred to be called George.

¤ Geoff Pullar, Lancashire's very successful Test batsman was nicknamed 'Noddy' because he could sleep anywhere and at any time.

¤ England coach David Lloyd was known as 'Bumble' because he talks incessantly with an engaging Lancashire burr.

Other players to be known by their nickname include, A.N. Hornby (Monkey), Harry Makepeace (Shake), Norman Oldfield (Buddy), Geoff Clayton (Chimp), Peter Lever (Plank), Barry Wood (Sawdust) and Graeme Fowler (Foxy).

NO-BALLS

There seems little doubt from the weight of contemporary evidence that Arthur Mold sometimes threw. Accusing fingers pointed in his direction and at Old Trafford in 1900, he was no-balled by umpire James Phillips, an Australian who had a reputation for toughness and had in the past 'called' Ernest Jones in Australia. For Mold, it was the beginning of the end. He was then left out of the side and had to watch his own benefit match against Yorkshire.

In 1901 when Lancashire met Somerset, Phillips was again the umpire. There was silence when Phillips first no-balled Mold, but as he continued to 'call' him, the anger of the crowd broke. Mold was no-balled eighteen times and police protection had to be sought for Phillips. Mold that day was no-balled out of cricket, yet it was claimed that cine shots of Mold bowling in the nets at Lord's showed that there was 'not a suggestion of a throw in his action'.

Phillips made many enemies during his time as an umpire, but he certainly had the courage to back his convictions!

NORTHAMPTONSHIRE

Founded in 1820, Northamptonshire have never won the County Championship, their best performance being second place, a position they have occupied four times. The county has won the Gillette Cup in 1976 and in 1992 under the title of the Nat West Trophy and the Benson and Hedges Cup in 1980.

In 1910, Lancashire had a remarkable victory at Northampton after they had scored 314 for five in just four hours play on the first two days and won by an innings and 112 runs when the home side were bowled out for 114 and 88. Jim Heap took 14 wickets, including nine for 43 in Northamptonshire's second innings.

Lancashire faced Northamptonshire in the opening match of their 1928 Championship-winning season and ran up a total of 528 for four in just under six hours with runs coming at 100 per hour after lunch. Frank Watson scored 233 in 245 minutes and shared in stands of 200 with Charlie Hallows for the first wicket and 179 in an hour and a half with Ernest Tyldesley for the second.

Northamptonshire were Lancashire's opponents when Ernest Tyldesley hit his 100th first-class century when the Red-Rose county won by an innings.

The match against Northamptonshire at Old Trafford on the final day of the 1951 season saw Lancashire needing 176 to win in 110 minutes. The last ball of the match was bowled with Lancashire 174 for eight. The batsman was Bob Berry, the bowler, former Lancashire player, Albert Nutter. Berry took a single but when the return came in, it was dropped by the wicket-keeper and the batsmen scrambled home for the second run and victory by two wickets.

Lancashire were red-hot favourites to lift the Gillette Cup when they met Northamptonshire in the 1976 Final, but even though David Hughes hit the left-arm spin of Indian Test player Bishen Bedi for 26 runs in the final over, Northamptonshire won by four wickets.

In 1996, Lancashire gained revenge by beating Northamptonshire by 31 runs in the Benson and Hedges Final. Lancashire's record of first-class matches v Northamptonshire is:

P.	W.	L.	D.	Tied
115	47	16	52	0

NOTTINGHAMSHIRE

Founded in 1841, Nottinghamshire were undoubtedly the strongest team in the country in the late 19th century, taking 10 unofficial county titles between 1865 and 1886. Since those days, the county have had occasional success, taking the Championship again in 1907, 1929, 1981 and 1987. They won their first one-day title in 1987 when they captured the Nat West Trophy and followed this up with the Benson and Hedges Cup in 1989 and the Sunday League in 1991.

J.T. Tyldesley scored the highest score of his career, 250 in the 1905 match at Trent Bridge. He had scored 156 when he was joined by last man Bill Worsley. The last pair added 141 in 85 minutes, taking Lancashire's score from 486 for nine to 627 all out, with what is the fourth highest last-wicket stand in history.

In 1910 at Old Trafford, Nottinghamshire had controlled the game for two days, setting Lancashire 400 to win in five and a quarter hours. After losing two early wickets, a third wicket partnership of 191 between J.T. Tyldesley and Jack Sharp set them on their way. They were 327 for five when Hornby, who had twisted his knee and was unable to bat in the first innings, strode to the wicket. He lost three partners and with their score on 364 for eight, it appeared that Lancashire's chances of winning had gone. But Lol Cook stayed with Hornby, who made 55 not out, to help Lancashire to a famous victory.

In 1926, Lancashire went into the last match against Nottinghamshire without captain Leonard Green and needing to win to lift the title. Nottinghamshire were dismissed for 292 and Harry Makepeace made 180 as Lancashire totalled 454. Nottinghamshire just managed to avoid an innings defeat, but Lancashire won by ten wickets to win the County Championship.

Lancashire were destroyed by the pace of Larwood and Voce in 1934, being dismissed for 119. Nottinghamshire led by 147 but after Ernest Tyldesley and Lionel Lister added 182 in 130 minutes, Lancashire were able to declare their second innings at 394 for seven. Nottinghamshire required 248 to win in two and three-quarter hours but with Hopwood spinning the ball viciously, Lancashire won by 101 runs. The Red-Rose all-rounder took six for 58 (ten for 157 in the match).

At Old Trafford in 1953, Roy Tattersall took nine for 40, seven of the wickets including the hat-trick, falling in nineteen balls without a run being scored!

In 1956, Lancashire captain Geoff Edrich declared after only one ball of the second innings. At the time, this was the shortest innings in history, but Nottinghamshire, set 98 to win in two hours, finished on 93 for seven when stumps were drawn.

In 1961, Lancashire beat Nottinghamshire at Worksop by six wickets. After only taking four Nottinghamshire wickets for 525 runs, Bob Barber scored 104 as Lancashire amassed 372 for four in five hours.

Lancashire's record of first-class matches v Nottinghamshire is:

P.	W.	L.	D.	Tied
213	64	49	100	0

OFFICE BLOCKS

Four Lancashire players (Archie MacLaren, Cyril Washbrook, George Duckworth and Brian Statham) have had office blocks near to the ground named after them, whilst Hornby and Barlow are remembered by roads named after them.

OLDEST

The oldest cricketer to appear for Lancashire is Albert Neilson Hornby who was 52 years 5 months old when he played his last game for the county against Leicestershire in 1899.

OLDFIELD, NORMAN

Norman Oldfield was on the Lancashire staff for six years before making his county debut in 1935. An entertaining stroke-maker he scored 1,066 runs in his first season, hitting undefeated hundreds against Hampshire at Aigburth and Leicestershire at Old Trafford.

Only 5ft 2 ins tall, Oldfield scored 1,000 runs in each of the seasons up to the outbreak of the Second World War, with a best of 1,823 at

42.13 in 1939. That summer he appeared for England against the West Indies at the Oval in what turned out to be the last Test match played before the hostilities. He scored 80 in the first innings and 19 in the second and looked to be on the verge of a long Test career.

When the war was over, Oldfield refused Lancashire's terms and joined Northamptonshire. Perhaps one of the most satisfying moments of his time with Northamptonshire was the century he scored against Lancashire on his return to Old Trafford with his new county.

Retiring from the first-class game in 1954, he had a spell umpiring before returning to Lancashire as assistant-coach, eventually succeeding Charlie Hallows as coach.

OLD TRAFFORD

Old Trafford has been the home of Lancashire cricket since 1857 when the new ground was opened. The county play the majority of their home matches at Old Trafford and of course the ground also stages Test matches and limited-overs international matches.

The first match staged there was between Manchester CC and Liverpool CC. The initial first-class match at the ground was between England and Another England XI in 1860. The first inter-county match was with Middlesex in 1865 when Vyell Walker took ten for 104 and both sides strangely scored 234 in their first innings. The first Test match was staged in 1884 when England played Australia.

The pavilion was built in 1894 and was used as a hospital during the First World War and was bombed during the Second World War. The rich history of the ground includes most of the greatest names in the game. There can be few who have not heard of 'Laker's Match'. An amazing spell of spin bowling gave the Surrey and England bowler ten Australian wickets in one innings for a cost of 53 runs and match figures of nineteen for 90, Laker taking all his wickets from the Stretford End.

The Old Trafford wicket has also confounded the experts. In 1952, India were dismissed for 58 and 82 inside a day, whilst six years later, Lancashire were shot out for 27 against Surrey. In 1964, Bobby Simpson scored 311 for Australia out of his side's total of 656 for eight, though the highest individual innings was played in 1996 when Jason Gallian made 312 against Derbyshire.

In 1971, the Gillette Cup semi-final match against Gloucestershire went on until nine o'clock, the lights on the Warwick Road Station blinding the players!

In more recent years, Viv Richards hit 189 not out in a Texaco Trophy match in 1984. Crowds at Old Trafford have always been large. The ground's record attendance was 78,617 for the Roses match in 1926 (46,000 attended on the first day) and for a limited-overs match, 33,000 against Yorkshire in the 1970 John Player League match.

ONE-DAY FINISHES

Lancashire have been involved in seven matches that have all been completed inside a day and have won six of them. Somerset have been their opponents on four of those occasions, with the last being June 1953.

Bertie Buse, the Somerset all-rounder had chosen this game at Bath as his Benefit match. Tattersall's first delivery turned two feet and cleared the batsman's head. Somerset were out for 55 just after one o'clock. Lancashire did better, scoring 150 with Marner and Wharton adding 70 for the sixth wicket in 25 minutes. Somerset's second innings lasted 13 balls fewer than their first and the game ended soon after 5.30pm. with Lancashire winning by an innings and 24 runs. The full list is:

v MCC	Lord's	Won by 6 wickets	1886
v Surrey	Old Trafford	Lost by an innings and 25 runs	1888
v Somerset	Old Trafford	Won by 8 wickets	1892
v Somerset	Old Trafford	Won by an innings and 68 runs	1894
v Somerset	Old Trafford	Won by 9 wickets	1925
v Sussex	Old Trafford	Won by an innings and 87 runs	1950
v Somerset	Bath	Won by an innings and 24 runs	1953

OPENERS

The only instance of a side winning a first-class match in England without losing a wicket occurred at Old Trafford in July 1956, when Lancashire scored 166 for 0 declared and 66 for 0, beating Leicestershire (108 and 122) by ten wickets. Alan Wharton (87* and 33*) and

Jack Dyson (75* and 31*) were the first pair of batsmen in all first-class cricket to monopolise totally their team's victory.

OVERSEAS PLAYERS

Lancashire have had a number of foreign-born players in their ranks prior to the influx of overseas players in the county game in the 1960s, with the most prominent being Australian pace bowler, Ted McDonald. He appeared in 11 Tests for his country before joining Lancashire in 1924 and taking 1,053 wickets at 20.96 in eight seasons. Another Australian-born cricketer to serve the county well was Ken Grieves who appeared in 452 matches between 1949 and 1964, scoring 20,802 runs, taking 235 wickets and holding 555 catches.

Other Australian Test players to play in a handful of games for the county include Ian Chappell, Geoff Lawson, Mick Malone and Chris Matthews. In the mid sixties, West Indian spin bowler Sonny Ramadhin played in 33 games for Lancashire, taking 97 wickets at 23.37 runs each.

In 1968, the game developed a new dimension with the introduction of immediately-registered overseas players. Lancashire missed out on Gary Sobers who went to Nottinghamshire but signed the Indian Test wicket-keeper/batsman Farokh Engineer and the exciting West Indian batsman Clive Lloyd who was playing professional with Haslingden in the Lancashire League and he became qualified for the 1969 season.

During the 1980s, West Indians Colin Croft, Michael Holding, Ken MacLeod and Patrick Patterson all played for Lancashire, as did Dane Soren Henriksen and South African Steve Jefferies.

New Zealand pace bowler Danny Morrison played for the county in 1992 whilst Lancashire's current overseas player Wasim Akram played the first of his 65 Championship matches in 1988.

OXFORD UNIVERSITY

One of the biggest hits ever seen at Old Trafford came in the 1883 match against Oxford University when Walter Robinson in his innings of 154 smashed a full length ball to square leg, over the flag post and clean out of the ground and on to the railway line.

In 1888, Lancashire pulled off a remarkable victory over Oxford University after being 93 for eight after following on 110 runs behind. The Red-Rose county eventually avoided the innings defeat and set the University 63 to win. Thinking victory was a certainty, the University reversed their batting order and lost by 20 runs!

The match against the University in 1890 was one of twelve-a-side but still regarded as first-class. Lancashire scored 138 and 142, the University 274, leaving them just seven to get for victory. This they achieved without losing a wicket, giving Lancashire the only eleven-wicket defeat in their history! Lancashire's record of first-class atches v Oxford University is

P.	W.	L.	D.	Tied
83	46	7	30	0

P

PAKISTAN

Pakistan were admitted to full Test status in July 1952 and two years later visited England for the first Test series between the two countries. When they met Lancashire in that summer of 1954, the Pakistan attack dismissed the Red-Rose side for 98, which is still the county's lowest score against the touring team. However, in the same match, Lancashire scored 324, which is their highest score against Pakistan. Lancashire's record of first-class matches v Pakistan is:

P.	W.	L.	D.	Tied
7	0	2	5	0

PARKIN, CECIL

Though he had played for Yorkshire in 1906, Cecil Parkin made his Lancashire debut in 1914 after a spell as professional with Church, the Lancashire League club. His first match was against Leicestershire at Aigburth, where he took fourteen for 99.

Unfortunately, the First World War interrupted his development and when cricket resumed in 1919, Parkin joined Rochdale as professional. Though he continued to play for Lancashire, he only

OGDEN'S CIGARETTES

C. H. PARKIN,
LANCASHIRE.

participated in 15 games in the first three years following the resumption of the game. Yet despite this, he was selected to tour Australia in the winter of 1920-21 with Johnny Douglas' team and though England lost all five Tests, Parkin was generally thought to be the best bowler in the England side. He played in all five Tests the following summer, taking 16 Australian wickets at a cost of 26.37 runs each.

Parkin was 36 years of age when in 1922 he finally became a full-time first-class cricketer with the county and in that season, took 181 wickets. The following season, he took 186 wickets for Lancashire and a year later 196 for Lancashire, over 200 in all matches.

Playing his final match for the county in 1926, Parkin took 901 wickets at 16.12 runs apiece in just 157 games. If he had devoted all his cricketing life to Lancashire, it is fairly certain that he would have set records that would still be standing today.

PAYNTER, EDDIE

Though Eddie Paynter played in half the games during the summer of 1930, he was in two minds at the end of it as to whether he should leave Old Trafford. Fortunately he decided to stay and fight for his place and in 1931 made the first of 20 appearances for England.

During the 1932-33 'Bodyline' tour of Australia, Paynter left his sick bed during the fourth Test at Brisbane to play a superb innings of 83 and guide England into a first innings lead. During the 1938 home series against Australia, Paynter finished the series with an average of over 100 after hitting 216 not out in the opening Test at Trent Bridge. In 1938-39, he scored hundreds in each innings of the Johannesburg Test and 243 in the third Test at Durban to finish with 653 runs at an average of 81.62, the highest aggregate for a series between England and South Africa.

Eddie Paynter

For Lancashire he scored 16,555 runs at an average of 41.59, including four double centuries and a treble. The treble hundred was made against Sussex at Hove in 1937 where his score of 322 was made in five hours out of Lancashire's total of 640 for eight.

Roses matches usually brought the best out of Eddie Paynter and his innings of 152 on a dangerous Bradford wicket in 1932 was superb. He had turned 44 when first-class cricket resumed after the war and he did not return to Old Trafford, preferring to play league cricket with Keighley in the Bradford League.

PERCENTAGES

In 1910, a new method of reckoning was introduced in the County Championship, as an experiment for one season. Teams were placed according to their 'percentage of wins' in all matches played, including draws. The new rule was proposed by Lancashire, who suffered most. Placed fourth that season, they would have been second under the previous method.

PHILLIPSON, EDDIE

Eddie Phillipson's career, like so many promising cricketers was marred by the outbreak of war in 1939. He had just taken 133 wickets at 22.33 runs each and made the highest score of his career, 113 against Glamorgan at Preston.

He had played his first game for Lancashire in 1933, and batting at Number 11, he took 27 runs off Sussex's Maurice Tate. The following season, he produced his best figures with the ball, taking eight for 100 against Kent at Dover.

His best season for Lancashire was 1937 when he took 131 wickets and missed the 'double' by just 134 runs, that after having missed the first seven matches of the season!

When the hostilities were over, he returned to Old Trafford but it was apparent that the war years had taken their toll and in 1948 he played his last game for the county. He took 545 wickets at 24.78 runs each and scored 4,050 runs at 25.96, a good average for a pace bowler.

Following his retirement from the playing side, he became a highly respected umpire, standing in 12 Tests between 1958 and 1965.

PILLING, HARRY

Standing just 5ft 2ins, Harry Pilling was the smallest man in the game and in 1966, four years after making his debut for Lancashire, he was awarded his county cap. He scored the first of his 25 centuries for Lancashire in 1963 when he made an unbeaten 133 against Hampshire in the match at Portsmouth. In the match against Warwickshire at Old Trafford in 1970, he made unbeaten centuries in both innings of the match and continued to produce a high standard of batsmanship until 1975 when loss of form, illness and injury began to curtail his appearances.

Harry Pilling

However, in 1976 he returned to top the county batting averages with 1,569 runs at an average of 52.30 and received wide support for a place in the England side to face the West Indies. A superb fielder, Harry Pilling played his last game in 1980 after scoring 14,841 runs at an average of 32.26.

PILLING, DICK

The 'Prince of Wicket-Keepers', Dick Pilling was born in Bedford of Lancashire parents and they returned to their native county and settled in Church. He soon joined the local cricket club and after impressing behind the stumps, was given a trial against Sussex in 1877 and never looked back.

By 1881, Pilling was regarded as the finest wicket-keeper in the country and in the winter of 1881-82 toured Australia where he made the first of his eight Test appearances.

As a batsman, Pilling made only two half-centuries for the county, one of them coming when he and Johnny Briggs shared in a last wicket stand of 173 against Surrey at Aigburth in 1885. It was at around this time that Pilling began to be ill and was frequently absent from the field.

He played the last of his 177 games for Lancashire in 1889 for towards the end of that year, he caught a heavy cold when playing football and was sent out to Australia at Lancashire's expense in an effort to make a complete recovery. He did improve slightly but within six days of his return to these shores, he had died of consumption. He held 333 catches and made 153 stumpings for Lancashire, a total of 486 victims.

PLACE, WINSTON

Winston Place made his debut for Lancashire in 1937, a season in which he took 137 off a Nottinghamshire attack spearheaded by Larwood and Voce at Trent Bridge. In 1939, the touring West Indians felt the full force of his stroke-play as he made 164 in a huge Lancashire total.

He overcame the loss of six vital summers to the hostilities to become Cyril Washbrook's regular opening partner. In 1947, he scored 2,408 runs at an average of 68.80 with a top score of 266 not out against Oxford University and was selected for the MCC tour of the Caribbean in 1947-48.

Though he failed in his early attempts on the tour, he scored a superb 107 in the final innings of the series at Kingston. The perfect foil to Washbrook, he scored 1,000 runs in each of the eight seasons after the war, ending his career in 1955 with 14,605 runs at an average of 36.69.

POLITICIANS

Five Lancashire cricketers have become Members of Parliament. They are Peter Eckersley, who led the county to the Championship in 1930 and 1934, Frank Hardcastle, Sir George Kemp, Sir Joseph Leese and Sir Lancelot Sanderson.

POLLARD, DICK

Like other Lancashire cricketers, the war years took a hefty slice from the career of Dick Pollard, who though he took 1,015 wickets for the county in a career that started in 1933, he could have surpassed the magnificent efforts of Statham and Briggs.

With the exception of the 1946 season, when he missed a number of matches while still serving in the forces, he took 100 wickets in a season on each occasion from 1936 to 1950. His best season was 1947 when he took 137 wickets for the county, while he performed the hat-trick on two occasions, against Glamorgan at Preston in 1939 and against Warwickshire at Blackpool in 1947.

He played in four Tests for England taking 15 wickets at 25.20 runs apiece, figures that suggest that the England selectors should have recognised Pollard's potential earlier. Known as 'Th'owd chain horse' due to his ability to bowl for long periods without complaining, he took 1,015 wickets for Lancashire at a cost of just 22.15 runs apiece.

PRESIDENTS

This is the complete list of the County's Presidents:

1873	Mark Phillips
1874-80	A.B. Rowley
1881-86	Sir H de Trafford
1887-93	Sir H.F. de Trafford
1894-1916	A.N. Hornby
1917-18	Lord Ellesmere
1919-20	Sir F. Hollins
1921-22	Lord Derby
1923-24	O.P. Lancashire
1925-26	Sir E. Stockton
1927-28	Lord Ashton
1929	Rev V.F. Royle
1930-31	Lord Derby
1932-33	Lord Colwyn
1934-35	Dr H.H.I. Hitchon
1936-37	M.N. Kenyon

(Presidents, contd.)

1938	Lord Stanley
1939-40	Sir T. Robinson
1941-42	Sir C. Needham
1943-44	Sir R. Noton Barclay
1945-46	R.H. Spooner
1947-48	W. Findlay
1949-50	Sir E. Rhodes
1951-52	Col L. Green
1953-54	T. Stone
1955-56	Dr J. Bowling Holmes
1957-58	Rt Hon Earl of Derby
1959-60	R.A. Boddington
1961-62	Stanley Holt
1963-64	Rev F. Paton-Williams
1965-66	J.S. Cragg
1967	G.O. Shelmerdine
1968	J.S. Cragg
1969-70	W.H. Lister
1971-72	Sir N. Cardus
1973-74	P. Higson
1975-76	F.D. Beattie
1977-78	T.A. Higson
1979-80	W.D. Crumblehulme
1981-82	J.L. Hopwood
1983-84	E. Kay
1985-86	C.D. Peaker
1987-88	B.J. Howard
1989-90	C. Washbrook
1991-92	A.J. Leggat
1993-94	K. Cranston
1995-96	B. Statham

PRESTON

The first county match played at Preston was in 1936 when the visitors were Gloucestershire. Boasting players of the calibre of Barnett, Goddard and Hammond, the visitors were dismissed for 138 with Hammond playing a fine innings of 65. Lancashire then collapsed to be bowled out for 45 before Gloucestershire in their second innings totalled 214. Lancashire were left a day and a half to get 307 for victory but despite a number of thunderstorms, the weather didn't save them and they lost by 175 runs late on the third day. The following year, the New Zealand tourists were well beaten by an innings and 74 runs with Iddon and Oldfield both scoring centuries.

In 1938, the Sussex game was badly affected by the rain and in 1939, Glamorgan were the opponents. The Welsh side were beaten by ten wickets with Dick Pollard performing the hat-trick and Eddie Phillipson hitting a career best 113.

The last first-class match played at the ground was in 1952, when Glamorgan were again the opponents. This time however, it was a drawn match, frequently interrupted by rain.

PULLAR, GEOFF

Geoff Pullar arrived at Old Trafford in 1954 and made his first-class debut that season against Surrey as a middle-order batsman before later progressing to Number 3. In 1957, he passed the 1,000 run mark for the first time; though his batting was improving, his fielding was not and in 1958 he was sent back from the Oval by Cyril Washbrook for not trying! Pullar buckled to and in three innings for the 2nd XI, two of them not out, he scored 199 runs. He returned immediately to the first team and after that, his place was never in doubt.

He began the summer of 1959 with seven consecutive innings of over fifty and he was chosen for England for the third Test at Headingley against India. Later that summer he became the first Lancashire player to score a century in a Test match at Old Trafford when he scored 131. After touring the Caribbean in 1959-60 were he scored 385 runs in the Tests at 42.77 he made a career highest 175 against the South Africans at the Oval. In the 1962-63 tour of Australia, he tore a cartilage and strained his groin. It was the end of his international career in which he had played in 28 Tests and scored 1,974 runs at an average of 43.86.

He continued to play for Lancashire until 1968, scoring 16,853 runs at 35.18 before leaving to join Gloucestershire. However, after just two seasons, his knee problems flared up again and after seeing a specialist, he was forced to retire.

RAINED OFF

The game arranged to take place at Aigburth between Lancashire and Kent on 4 – 6 June 1891, was completely rained off, the first time in the County Championship that this happened.

RECORD WICKET PARTNERSHIPS

The county's highest partnerships for each wicket is as follows:

1st	368	A.C. MacLaren/R.Spooner	v Gloucestershire at Liverpool 1903
2nd	371	F. Watson/E.Tyldesley	v Surrey at Old Trafford 1928
3rd	364	M. Atherton/N.Fairbrother	v Surrey at The Oval 1990
4th	324	A.C. MacLaren/J.T.Tyldesley	v Nottinghamshire at Trent Bridge 1904
5th	249	B. Wood/A.Kennedy	v Warwickshire at Edgbaston 1975
6th	278	J. Iddon/H. Butterworth	v Sussex at Old Trafford 1932
7th	245	A.H. Hornby/J.Sharp	v Leicestershire at Old Trafford 1912
8th	158	J. Lyon/B. Ratcliffe	v Warwickshire at Old Trafford 1979
9th	142	L. Poidevin/A. Kermode	v Sussex at Eastbourne 1907
10th	173	J. Briggs/R.Pilling	v Surrey at Liverpool 1885

REYNOLDS, FRED

Educated at Cambridge University and Charterhouse, he later became one of the Lord's ground bowlers before playing for Suffolk and George Parr's England Eleven. In 1860, he joined Manchester Cricket Club and then played in the county's first match in 1865 until 1874. All told, he played in 38 games, taking 94 wickets at 19.39 runs each.

After his playing days were over, he became the Old Trafford ground manager, a position he held until his retirement at the age of 74 in 1908.

RICKETTS, JIM

One of the few Lancashire-born professionals to make his mark in county cricket in the early years of the game, he played his first game for Lancashire against Surrey at the Oval in 1867. He opened the batting and carried his bat for 195 not out to achieve what in those days was an incredible feat. He only played in 33 matches over the next ten years and passed the fifty mark on just one occasion to finish with 1,120 runs at an average of 18.06.

ROWLEY, EDMUND

Although missing the county's first match against Middlesex when his brother Alexander Butler Rowley captained the side, he was appointed the first official captain of Lancashire. Educated at Rossall, he represented the Gentlemen against the Players in 1862 and in 1867, scored 219 out of a total of 586 when playing for the Gentlemen of Lancashire against the Gentlemen of Yorkshire. That summer also saw his highest score for Lancashire when he made 78 against Surrey at The Oval.

He captained Lancashire for 14 years, leading the side to share the County Championship with Nottinghamshire in 1879.

ROYLE, VERNON

One of the finest cover-point fielders the game has ever seen, Vernon Royle first played for Lancashire against Yorkshire in 1873. His debut was quite unique in that he was bowled first ball in each innings by Allen Hill!

For Lancashire he scored 1,754 runs at an average of 15.66 and failed to score a century in his 74 matches, although he ended the 1878 season in second place in the county batting averages. However, in 1874, he scored 205 for the Gentlemen of Cheshire against Staffordshire Borderers at Chelford.

Though he only took two wickets for Lancashire, when he was at Oxford University, he developed a talent for slow bowling and in the Varsity game of 1875, dismissed four of the first five Cambridge batsmen in a game Oxford won by six runs. It was for his fielding though that Vernon Royle will be remembered. Ambidextrous and quick on his feet, he toured Australia in 1878-79 with Lord Hawke's team and though he only played in one Test, he held five catches at cover-point.

A master at Elstree School, he was ordained in 1881 and became curate at Aldenham near Watford and though he intended to become involved in parish work, he stayed on at Elstree, where his duties forced him to give up first-class cricket.

RUGBY LEAGUE

Whilst there are no Lancashire cricketers who were double internationals, Alan Wharton, who appeared in one Test for England against New Zealand in 1949, came close when playing for Salford and Broughton Park.

RUGBY UNION

The first double international at cricket and rugby union was A.N. 'Monkey' Hornby. He made three appearances for England at cricket between 1879 and 1884, his first against Australia at Melbourne on 2 – 4 January 1879. He played nine times for England at Rugby Union between 1877 and 1882. He was also the first man to captain England at both sports, both of which he did in 1882, at rugby v Scotland and at cricket v Australia at The Oval, when Australia achieved their first win in England and as a result of which the Ashes came into being. Reginald Spooner was also a double international, whilst Arthur Paul toured Australia with the British Isles Rugby Union side in 1888.

RUNNER

The only batsman to score hundreds in each innings of a first-class match with the aid of a runner is Lancashire's Graeme Fowler at Southport on 28-30 July 1982. He strained a thigh muscle while fielding during Warwickshire's record fourth-wicket stand of 470 on the first day. Opening Lancashire's reply, he scored 26 before adding a further 100 with a runner. His scores of 126 and 128 not out enabled Lancashire to win a remarkable match by ten wickets. When he completed his second century, his runner had his hand shaken by a fielder and waved his bat to acknowledge the applause.

S

SEMI-FINALS

Up to the end of the 1996 season, Lancashire had appeared in 27 semi-finals of limited-overs competitions, comprising of 14 Gillette Cup/Nat West Trophy, 9 Benson and Hedges Cup and four appearances in the Refuge Assurance Cup.

SHARP, JACK

In a county career that spanned twenty-seven years, Jack Sharp scored 22,015 runs at an average of 31.18 and took 434 wickets at a cost of 27.23 runs each. He made his debut for Lancashire in 1899 in a match against Surrey at Old Trafford, hitting one ball over the sight-screen and another into the covered stand near the entrance to the pavilion.

In his early days with the county, he was considered more of a bowler and in 1901, took 113 wickets including a career best nine for 77 against Worcestershire. But it was as a batsman that Jack Sharp was to become known and, over the coming years, he passed 1,000 runs a season on ten occasions with a best of 2,099 runs in all matches in 1911.

A celebrated footballer, he played for Aston Villa, Everton and England and appeared in successive FA Cup Finals for the Goodison Park club. He also played in three Test matches for England, scoring 61 on his debut and 105 in his final match against the 1909 Australian side to finish with a Test average of 47.00.

COUNTY CRICKETERS.

J. SHARP,
LANCASHIRE.

For Lancashire, he scored 38 centuries with a highest of 211 against Leicestershire at Old Trafford in 1912. In 1923, at the age of 45, Sharp was appointed captain of Lancashire – a fitting tribute to one of the county's finest all-rounders. He retired two years later, becoming the first former professional cricketer to become a Test selector.

SHUTTLEWORTH, KEN

He made his Lancashire debut in the summer of 1964 in the Roses game at Old Trafford, taking the wicket of Geoff Boycott. However, he took a while to establish himself at Old Trafford and it was 1968 before he was awarded his county cap.

His best season for the county was 1970 when he took 74 wickets at 21.60 runs apiece. This summer also saw him play for England against The Rest of the World at Lord's and at the end of the season

he toured Australia with Ray Illingworth's side. He took five for 47 at Brisbane and played in four of the Tests. His final appearance for England came against Pakistan in 1971, his 12 wickets costing 35.58 runs each.

His best figures for Lancashire were seven for 41 against Essex at Leyton but in 1975 after a career plagued with injuries, he played his last game for the county. Having taken 484 wickets at 22.92 runs each, he moved to Grace Road to end his career with Leicestershire.

Ken Shuttleworth

SIMMONS, JACK

Jack Simmons was 19 years old when he was asked to join the Lancashire ground staff but he turned down the request in order to finish his apprenticeship as a draughtsman. He was told he would be invited again in two years time, but the invitation never came and he settled down to a life as a league professional, initially in the Ribblesdale League. He was with Blackpool in 1968 when Buddy Oldfield asked him again to play for Lancashire's 2nd XI.

Jack Simmons

He made his first team debut against Northamptonshire that summer but 1969 was his first full season of first-class cricket – he was 29 years of age. In 1970, he scored his first century for the county after coming in as night-watchman against Sussex at Hove. That summer also saw him acquire the nickname of 'Flat Jack' as he pushed the ball through with a flat trajectory.

Over the years, he continued to improve with age and helped the county to win the Sunday League in 1969 and 1970 and the Gillette Cup in 1970, 1971, 1972 and 1975. In 1979, he led Tasmania into the Sheffield Shield and won the Gillette Cup Final for them with an all-round display that won him the Man-of-the-Match Award as he took four for 17 and made 55 not out.

Aged 48, he decided to retire at the end of the 1989 season, having taken 985 wickets at 26.89 runs apiece and scored 8,773 runs at an average of 22.61. One of the most popular players in the county's history, he currently serves on the Lancashire Committee.

SINGLE HIT

The most runs scored from a single hit in any first-class match is ten. The record was set at The Oval on 14 July 1873 when Lancashire's opening batsman A.N. Hornby, whose score of 20 was the highest of the county's total of 100, made half his runs off a single delivery from Surrey's James Street.

SIXES

Frank Hayes playing against Glamorgan at Swansea in 1977, hit 34 runs (five sixes and a four) off a six-ball Malcolm Nash over. Nash was also the sufferer when Gary Sobers hit 36 off an over. The umpire on that occasion was former Lancashire bowler, Eddie Phillipson. Sobers' record has since been equalled by Ravi Shastri, the only time that Hayes' feat has been beaten.

SOMERSET

Founded in 1875, Somerset went over 100 years without winning a trophy, before they won five one-day titles; the Benson and Hedges

Cup in 1981 and 1982, the 1979 Gillette Cup and Sunday League and the Nat West Trophy in 1983. When the two sides met at Old Trafford in 1882, the game provided a piece of history as Lancashire won by an innings and 157 runs. Somerset were bowled out for 29 and 51 with George Nash taking four wickets in four balls in Somerset's first innings of which seven players failed to score!

In 1895, Archie MacLaren scored 424 in ten minutes short of eight hours in the match at Taunton, a score that remained the highest individual innings played in England until Brian Lara's 501 not out for Warwickshire against Durham in 1994.

Lancashire's total of 580 against Somerset at Old Trafford in 1904 was the highest in a county match in Lancashire at the time. It was also the only occasion in the county's history when an innings included four separate centuries – Cuttell, A.H. Hornby, MacLaren and J.T. Tyldesley being the batsmen.

In 1905, Somerset visited Old Trafford and were bowled out for 65 in an hour and a quarter with Walter Brearley taking nine for 47. Hornby then hit a hundred in 43 minutes, Lancashire's fastest century until O'Shaughnessy's equalling of the world record in 1983. Somerset played better in their second innings but with Brearley taking eight for 90 they failed to avoid defeat. Brearley's performance is still Lancashire's only seventeen wicket haul in the County Championship.

When the two sides met at Bath in 1953, the game was over in a day. With Roy Tattersall opening the bowling, Somerset were all out for 55 and Lancashire themselves were struggling at 46 for five until 17-year-old Peter Marner hit a quick-fire 44, enabling Lancashire to score 158. Bowling unchanged, Tattersall had match figures of thirteen for 69 as Somerset were bowled out for 79. Bertie Buse, the Somerset medium-pace bowler had taken six for 41 in Lancashire's innings but he was an unhappy man, for this was his benefit match!

Lancashire's record of first-class matches v Somerset is:

P.	W.	L.	D.	Tied
132	72	22	38	0

SOUTH AFRICA

The first South African team visited England in 1894, but no Tests were played and the tourists were not accorded first-class status. When they did play their first Test series in this country in 1907, they played Lancashire at Old Trafford and scored 429, their highest score in this fixture.

In 1912, South Africa, who lost all three Tests against England, were dismissed for 44 at Aigburth, their lowest total in matches against Lancashire, yet still hung on for a draw. Lancashire's highest score against the South African tourists came in 1924 when they amassed 445 for six in the match at Old Trafford, whilst they were dismissed for just 90 in the 1960 match at Blackpool.

Lancashire's record of first-class matches v South Africa is:

P.	W.	L.	D.	Tied
17	5	3	9	0

SOUTHPORT

The first county match allocated to the ground was in 1959 when Lancashire played Worcestershire on 22, 24, 25 August. In 1967, due to the waterlogged state of the Old Trafford ground, the fixture against the Indian tourists was at the last minute switched to Southport and the drawn game was watched by almost 6,000 paying spectators in addition to members.

A truly remarkable match took place at Southport in 1982 when Lancashire played Warwickshire. In their first innings, the Warwickshire batsmen destroyed the Lancashire bowling, declaring before the end of the first day's play at 523 for four with Alvin Kallicharran 230 not out and Geoff Humpage 254, adding 470 runs in 290 minutes.

Lancashire declared at 414 for six with Graeme Fowler 126 and then bowled out the Warwickshire side for 111 with Les McFarlane taking six for 59. Then on the third afternoon, the Lancashire batsmen knocked off the 226 runs needed without losing a wicket, with Graeme Fowler 128 not out. Fowler batted through both innings with the aid of a runner, having been injured on the first day.

SPOONER, REG

COUNTY CRICKETERS.

MR. R. H. SPOONER,
LANCASHIRE.

Born at Litherland, near Liverpool, Marlborough educated Reg Spooner was invited to play for the county of his birth and in 1899 played his first game for Lancashire against Middlesex at Lord's, scoring 44 and 83. He was unable to play for Lancashire between 1900 and 1902 for, after fighting in the Boer War, he was stationed with the militia in Ireland. His business commitments then reduced drastically the time he could devote to the game and he was only able to play on a regular basis for six seasons. In 1910, he scored 200 not out against Yorkshire at Old Trafford, still the highest score made by a Lancashire player in Roses matches.

Reg Spooner first played for England in the Old Trafford Test of 1905, scoring 52 in a match the Australians lost by an innings. He was asked to captain the 1920-21 England side to tour Australia but again business prevented him from doing so. It seems such a sad waste that Spooner, one of the loveliest of stroke players, only played in ten Test matches, scoring 481 runs at an average of 32.06.

He played a number of times for the Gentlemen v Players and in 1906, scored 114 at Lord's, an innings rated one of the greatest in these annual encounters. One of the greatest cover fielders of his day, he scored 9,889 runs for Lancashire at an average of 37.17 and was the Club's President in 1945 and 1946.

SRI LANKA

It was on 17 February 1982 that a Sri Lankan team met England at Colombo in the first full Test match played by this island some half the size of England. Lancashire and Sri Lanka have met on two occasions, both of which have ended in a draw. At Old Trafford in 1990, Mahanama and Jayasuriya both scored hundreds, whilst Graham Lloyd hit a superb 96 from only 87 balls. Lancashire's record of first-class matches v Sri Lanka is:

P.	W.	L.	D.	Tied
2	0	0	2	0

STATHAM, BRIAN

One of the all-time greats, Brian Statham first played for Lancashire in 1950 and between then and his final game in 1968, he took 1,816 wickets for the county at 15.12 runs each.

Following his demobilization from the RAF, Statham made his county debut against Kent on his twentieth birthday. However, it was later that season that he made people sit up and take notice. In the Roses match at Old Trafford he took five for 52, including Lester, Lowson and Watson in an opening spell of three for 13. The following winter, he was flown out as one of the replacements for Freddie Brown's injury ravaged side and played the first of his 70 Test matches against New Zealand.

In 1951, his first full season in county cricket, he took 97 wickets and topped the Lancashire bowling averages for the first of fifteen occasions. After proving himself a first-rate Test bowler in the Caribbean in 1953-54, he teamed up with Frank Tyson the following winter in Australia to form one of the all-time great bowling combinations.

Then in the 1955 home series against South Africa, in which Tyson could not play, Statham took seven for 39 at Lord's to bring England a victory that at one time had seemed impossible.

His career in county and international cricket continued over the years. He got through a tremendous amount of hard work and bowled so fast and straight that batsmen could not afford to take liberties with him. He captained Lancashire for three years from 1965 to 1967 and played his last match for the county in 1968 in the Old Trafford Roses match. He was then 38 years old but took six for 34 as Yorkshire were skittled out for 61. Awarded the CBE in 1966 for his services to the game, he is currently the President of the County Club.

STEEL, ALLAN

Considered second only to W.G. Grace as the country's finest all-rounder, he first played for Lancashire in 1877 and though he last played for the county in 1893, he only appeared in 47 games.

On leaving Marlborough, he made his county debut against Sussex at Old Trafford, scoring 87 before entering Cambridge University. In his first match for Cambridge he took eight for 95 against an Eleven of England. For Lancashire in 1878, he took fourteen for 112 against

Brian Statham

Yorkshire, including his best innings analysis of nine for 63. In the Roses match of 1881, the Liverpool-born all-rounder scored 57 and 3 not out and took thirteen for 146.

Playing for the MCC against Yorkshire in 1881 he scored a magnificent 106 and though in his career, he was to reach three figures on eight occasions, only once did he achieve the feat for Lancashire.

A man for the big occasion, he played in 13 Tests for England, scoring 135 in Sydney in 1883 and 148 at Lord's a year later. One of four brothers who played for Lancashire, he scored 1,960 runs at an average of 29.25 and took 238 wickets at 13.16 runs each.

SUGG, FRANK

Derbyshire-born Frank Sugg played for Yorkshire and then his native county, for whom he scored 187 against Hampshire before joining  Lancashire in 1887. The following season, he played in two Tests for England at The Oval and Old Trafford, both of which were won. This season of 1888 also saw him score his first century for Lancashire when he made 102 not out on a difficult wicket at Gloucester Spa. In fact, three of Sugg's five centuries for Lancashire were against Gloucestershire with his highest-ever score of 220 made at Bristol in 1896.

Frank Sugg was an all-round sportsman, playing football for Sheffield Wednesday, Derby County, Burnley and Bolton Wanderers and was noted for his long-distance swimming, putting the shot, weight-lifting and reaching the final of the Liverpool amateur billiards championships.

SUNDAY LEAGUE

The John Player League was first contested in 1969. The then seventeen first-class counties played 40 over matches on a league basis, the format remaining unchanged until 1988, when a final first decided the championship. New sponsors, Refuge Assurance took over in 1987, followed by Axa Equity and Law in 1993.

The first set of matches were played on 27 April 1969 and the winners in that first season were Lancashire, by one point from Hampshire. The county won the League again the following year and again in 1989, when Paul Allott hit a six off the first ball of the last over against Surrey at Old Trafford to clinch victory and the Refuge Assurance Trophy. The county's records in those Championship seasons was as follows:

	P.	W.	L.	Tie	No Result	Points
1969	16	12	3	0	1	49
1970	16	13	2	0	1	53
1989	16	12	2	0	2	52

In 1988, Lancashire finished in third place after winning ten of their matches. This sent the county to Gloucestershire for the semi-final play-offs. Excellent bowling saw the home side restricted to 117 for nine with Paul Allott taking two for 14 off his eight overs. Lancashire looked home and dry at 77 for two, but Gloucestershire hit back to leave Man-of-the-Match Paul Allott to win the tie off his bat.

A full house at Edgbaston saw Lancashire beat Worcestershire in the first ever Refuge Assurance Cup Final. Lancashire lost Mendis and Hayhurst with only four on the board but rallied to end their forty overs on 201 for five. Andy Hayhurst took four for 46 as Worcestershire were dismissed for 149.

Lancashire's full record in the Sunday League is as follows:

P.	W.	L.	Tie	No Result	Abandoned
453	228	167	9	31	18

Other Sunday League records include:

Highest Innings Total	300 v Leicestershire at Leicester in 1993
Lowest Completed Innings Total	71 v Essex at Chelmsford in 1987
Highest Individual Innings	134* by C. Lloyd v Somerset at Old Trafford in 1970
Best Bowling Performance	6 for 29 by D. Hughes v Somerset at Old Trafford in 1977
Highest Partnership	182 for 3rd wicket by H. Pilling and C. Lloyd v Somerset at Old Trafford in 1970
Most Runs in a Season	773 by G. Fowler in 1990
Most Wickets in a Season	29 by Wasim Akram in 1995

SURREY

Founded in 1845, Surrey won three unofficial titles before capturing the first official County Championship in 1890. The county have won fifteen Championships altogether, including an unprecedented run of seven successive wins from 1952 to 1958. Their last Championship came in 1971. The county have also won all the one-day competitions, winning the Benson and Hedges Cup in 1974, the Nat West Trophy in 1982 and the Sunday League in 1996.

When Lancashire played Surrey at the Oval in 1866, Roger Iddison scored the county's first century. His innings of 106 was made up of two 4s, five 3s, eighteen 2s and forty seven singles. In 1885, Johnny Briggs and wicket-keeper Dick Pilling shared in a record last-wicket stand of 173 in the match against Surrey at Aigburth.

The first of Lancashire's three tied matches came against Surrey at the Oval in 1894. On a difficult wicket, Lancashire needed 75 for victory, but lost their first five wickets with just 9 on the board and then became 26 for seven. Two Yorkshire-born professionals, Tinsley and Smith took the score to 63 before Smith was out. Bardswell joined Tinsley but refused to run four off a big hit which would have left Lancashire level with two wickets to fall. He was out next ball and in the next over Tinsley offered a catch that was dropped and the batsmen ran a single to tie the scores. Mold was given out two balls later, caught at the wicket, but he always maintained that he never touched it!

When the teams met at the Oval in August 1897, Lancashire were top of the table with Surrey second and closing fast. It seemed that whoever won this match would win the title as well. Tom Richardson, Surrey's fast bowler, destroyed the Lancashire batting, laying out MacLaren and breaking the bats of Sugg and Ward as well as the former's finger. Other batsmen were hit and J.T. Tyldesley faced one over in which every ball sped past him at head height. Lancashire lost by six wickets but did win the title after Surrey failed to beat Somerset in their last match.

At the Oval in 1898, Tom Hayward made the only treble century that has been scored against Lancashire. His innings of 315 not out taking him six and three-quarter hours.

In 1926, Lancashire pulled off a most unlikely victory over Surrey in the match at Old Trafford as they went on to win the title. Surrey needed 159 to win in two and a half hours and at tea required just 58 with seven wickets standing. Jack Hobbs was then stumped and wickets fell steadily until Surrey reached 124 for nine. Dick Tyldesley then had Stan Fenley leg-before with the last ball of the match and Lancashire had won a great game of cricket by 34 runs.

Lancashire's record of first-class matches v Surrey is:

P.	W.	L.	D.	Tied
195	54	58	82	1

SUSSEX

Founded in 1839, Sussex have seven times been Championship runners-up but have never managed to win the title. The county won the first two Gillette Cups and also won the same cup in 1978, the Sunday League in 1982 and the Nat West Trophy in 1986.

When Lancashire played Sussex at Old Trafford in 1869, the Reverend Frank Wright, the man who had pulled out of the first Lancashire game in 1865 and was making only his second appearance for the county, scored 120, the first-ever century by a Lancashire player at Old Trafford.

When the two counties met in 1890, Lancashire declared for the first time in a rain-affected match. There was no play on the first day and after a start had been made just before lunch on the second day, Lancashire were 246 for two when play ended. There was an undefeated stand of 215 between Johnny Briggs and Albert Ward, which at the time was the second highest in the county's history. Play could not start until 2.50pm. on the last day when Arthur Kemble, captaining the side in Pilling's absence immediately declared. Sussex were then bowled out for 35 and following-on, were dismissed for 24, to give Lancashire victory by an innings and 187 runs. Johnny Briggs took five for 16 in Sussex's second innings, with all five wickets coming in seven balls! Also that summer, Archie MacLaren made his Lancashire debut against Sussex in the return match at Brighton. He scored 108, only the second player for the county to score a century on his first-class debut.

When the two sides met at Old Trafford in 1897, Johnny Briggs bowled 126 five-ball overs, taking two for 174 and 2 for 132. Bowling

630 balls, he conceded 306 runs, both of which are records for a County Championship match.

When Lancashire played Sussex at Hove in 1935, they scored 640 for eight on the opening day. It is the highest number of runs achieved by the county in a day and the second highest in county cricket. Eddie Paynter who didn't arrive at Hove until 8 o'clock in the morning because he had been playing at Old Trafford in a Test match, scored 322. His innings, second only to MacLaren's 424 contained three sixes and 39 fours. Lancashire won by an innings and five runs after a brave fight by Sussex to make the Red-Rose county bat again. Lancashire's record of first-class matches v Sussex is:

P.	W.	L.	D.	Tied
181	72	40	69	0

T

TATTERSALL, ROY

Roy Tattersall made his debut for Lancashire in 1948 as a medium-pace bowler but was persuaded by coach Harry Makepeace to try off spin and in 1950, his first full year as a spinner, he took 163 wickets in the Championship and 193 in all matches at 13.59 runs apiece.

Between 1951 and 1954, the Bolton-born bowler played 16 times for England, taking 58 wickets at 26.18 and a best of seven for 52 against South Africa at Lord's in 1951. In 1952, he took 145 wickets at 17.70 runs each and the following year 164 wickets. In that 1953 season he had the match analysis of fourteen for 73 against Nottinghamshire at Old Trafford, including the hat-trick. Though he played his last Test in 1954, he continued to be an important member of the Lancashire side and that summer took 117 wickets and in 1955, 124 wickets on pitches that were better suited to batsmen.

He continued to bowl well for the county but towards the end of the summer of 1958 he was left out of the side and it seemed as if his career at Old Trafford was coming to an end. So it proved for in 1960, he played the last of his 277 matches, having taken 1,168 wickets at 17.39 runs each.

TEST CRICKETERS

Lancashire's most capped player is Clive Lloyd, who won 110 caps for the West Indies. The full list is as follows:

England

P. Allott	13	C. Parkin	10
M. Atherton	67	E. Paynter	20
R. Barber	28	R. Pilling	8
R. Barlow	17	W. Place	3
S. Barnes	27	R. Pollard	4
R. Berry	2	G. Pullar	28
W. Brearley	4	V. Royle	1
J. Briggs	33	S. Schultz	1
K. Cranston	8	J. Sharp	3
J. Crawley	16	K. Shuttleworth	5
W. Cuttell	2	R. Spooner	10
H. Dean	3	B. Statham	70
P. de Freitas	44	A. Steel	13
G. Duckworth	24	F. Sugg	2
N. Fairbrother	10	R. Tattersall	16
W. Farrimond	4	E. Tyldesley	14
G. Fowler	21	J.T. Tyldesley	31
J. Gallian	3	R. Tyldesley	7
T. Greenhough	4	A. Ward	7
C. Hallows	2	C. Washbrook	37
F. Hayes	9	M. Watkinson	4
K. Higgs	15	A. Wharton	1
M. Hilton	4	L. Wilkinson	3
L. Hopwood	2	B. Wood	12
A.N. Hornby	3	R. Wood	1
N. Howard	4	**India**	
J. Iddon	5	F. Engineer	46
J. Ikin	18	**Pakistan**	
P. Lever	17	Wasim Akram	50
D. Lloyd	9	**West Indies**	
A. MacLaren	35	C. Croft	27
P. Martin	6	C. Lloyd	110
A. Mold	3	P. Patterson	28
N. Oldfield	1		

The first Lancashire players to appear in a Test match were A.N. Hornby, Vernon Royle, and Sandford Schultz who played for England v Australia in Melbourne in 1879.

THOUSAND RUNS

¤ In 1928, Charlie Hallows scored 1,000 runs in May, equalling W.G. Grace's record as Wally Hammond had done the previous season.

¤ Ernest Tyldesley in 1926 and Cyril Washbrook in 1946 achieved this feat in all first-class matches in July.

¤ Neil Fairbrother scored exactly 1,000 runs in all competitions in May 1990 – County Championship 674, Refuge Assurance 125, and Benson and Hedges Cup 201 runs.

¤ The first player to score 1,000 runs in a season for Lancashire was A.N. Hornby in 1881, when he scored 1,002 runs at 50.10.

TIED MATCHES

Lancashire have been involved in three tied matches, though the match against an England XI at Blackpool in 1905 is generally reckoned a tie, but Lancashire had three wickets to fall when the game ended.

The first tied match came in 1894 at the Oval when Lancashire left 75 to score for victory, collapsed to 26 for seven after losing their first five wickets for nine runs. With two runs required and the last pair at the wicket, Tinsley offered a catch which would have given Surrey the win, but the chance was not taken and the two batsmen scampered a single only for Mold to be given out caught behind next ball!

Hampshire were Lancashire's opponents in the next tied match, played at Bournemouth in 1947. Washbrook and Place opened with a stand of 142 in 90 minutes towards the 221 runs needed to win, but Alf Barlow, Lancashire's last man was run out in the final over when going for the winning run!

Lancashire's third tied match came against Essex at Brentwood in 1952. Needing 232 to win, Essex reached the last over needing nine and the last two batsmen together. Trevor Bailey hit Hilton's first ball for six, ran two off the second, when he was dropped on the boundary and then fell to an excellent catch by Nigel Howard when the scores were level!

TWO HUNDRED WICKETS IN A SEASON

This feat has been achieved by three Lancashire players but on five occasions and includes all first-class matches:

	For Lancashire			All First-Class Matches	
	Year	Wkts	Av.	Wkts	Av.
A. Mold	1894	189	11.84	207	12.30
A. Mold	1895	192	13.73	213	15.96
C. Parkin	1923	186	16.06	209	16.94
C. Parkin	1924	194	13.38	200	13.67
T. McDonald	1925	198	18.55	205	18.67

TWO THOUSAND RUNS

The first batsman to score 2,000 runs in a season for Lancashire was J.T. Tyldesley in 1901, when he scored 2,633 at 56.02. The highest number of runs scored in any one season for the county is Eddie Paynter's 2,727 at 58.35 in 1937. The batsman with the highest average is Ernest Tyldesley who scored 2,467 runs in 1928 at an average of 77.09.

In all matches in 1965, David Green scored 2,037 runs at an average of 32.85, without hitting a century, the only batsman to pass the landmark without recording a three-figure score.

TYLDESLEY, ERNEST

Though he made his debut for Lancashire in 1909, scoring 61 against Warwickshire at Aigburth, it wasn't until after the First World War that his true batting ability was revealed. He scored more runs for the county at a better average than any other batsman – 34,222 at 45.20, yet he did not play for England as often as his ability warranted. He played in 14 Test matches and scored 990 runs at an average of 55.00 with a highest score of 122, made against South Africa at Johannesburg in 1927-28 and against the West Indies at Lord's the following summer.

Ernest Tyldesley

For Lancashire he scored 90 centuries, twice making a hundred in each innings of a county match. His highest score was 256 not out against Warwickshire at Old Trafford in 1930. He passed 1,000 runs in a season on nineteen occasions with a best of 2,467 at 77.09 in 1928. In the summer of 1926 between 26 June and 6 August, he scored 1,477 runs in thirteen innings including eight centuries – a remarkable sequence.

The senior professional of the Lancashire side that won the County Championship three years in succession in 1926, 1927 and 1928, he played his last game for the county in 1936.

TYLDESLEY, JOHNNY

Though he did not score as many runs as his younger brother Ernest, J.T. as he was known, was thought to be the superior of the two. After scoring 33 in his first innings for the county against Gloucestershire at Old Trafford in 1895, he scored 152 not out against Warwickshire at Edgbaston in his next game. He again showed a liking for the Edgbaston wicket in 1897 when he scored a century in each innings of the game. However, it was the summer of 1898 when J.T. Tyldesley can be said to have arrived. He almost scored 2,000 runs in all first-class matches and made his first double century, 200 against Derbyshire at Old Trafford.

In 1899, he made the first of his 31 appearances for England in which he scored 1,661 runs at 30.75 with a highest score of 138 against Australia at Edgbaston in 1902. Though there are batsmen who have made more runs and at a better average, it has to be remembered that all Tyldesley's appearances were against top-class opposition on indifferent wickets.

J.T. Tyldesley

For Lancashire, he scored 31,949 runs at an average of 41.38, including hundreds against each one of the counties then playing first-class cricket. His highest score was 295 made against Kent at Old Trafford in 1906. Along with Archie MacLaren he holds the Lancashire record fourth wicket partnership of 324 against Nottinghamshire at Trent Bridge in 1904.

When cricket resumed after the hostilities, J.T. would have sooner retired, but he was persuaded to play for one more season in which he scored over 1,000 runs for the nineteenth season in succession and hit three centuries, the highest being 272 against Derbyshire. He did play in one more match in 1923, when he was the county's coach and was asked to captain the side in place of the injured Jack Sharp.

TYLDESLEY, DICK

Though he was not related to J.T. and Ernest Tyldesley, he was one of four brothers to play for Lancashire. Arriving at Old Trafford in 1919, he played for the county until 1931, in which time he had taken 1,449 wickets at a cost of 16.65 runs each, an aggregate that had only been bettered by Briggs and Mold until the arrival of Brian Statham.

His best season for the county was 1924 when he took 167 wickets at a cost of 13.32 runs each, including six for 18 in the Roses match at Headingley when Yorkshire were bowled out for 33 in their second

innings to give Lancashire victory by 24 runs. Also that summer he took seven for 6 against Northamptonshire but his best figures for the county were also against Northamptonshire at Kettering in 1926 when he took eight for 15. He appeared in seven Test matches for England, his penultimate appearance at Trent Bridge in 1930 causing him to miss his own benefit match!

A disagreement over terms at the end of the 1931 season took Dick Tyldesley away from Old Trafford when he still had several more seasons use to the county in him.

U

UNDEFEATED

Lancashire have gone through a County Championship season without losing a game on four occasions. In 1904, the county won the Championship, winning 16 and drawing 10 of its matches. In 1928, the county won the Championship, winning 15 and drawing 15 of its 30 matches. In 1930, Lancashire won 10 of its 28 matches in winning the County Championship, whilst the last time they achieved the feat was 1974 when they won 5 of their 20 matches and finished the season in eighth place.

UMPIRES

Since the Second World War, eight Lancashire players have become first-class umpires. They are Jack Bond, John Bowes, David Lloyd, Eddie Paynter, Winston Place, Harry Elliott, Norman Oldfield and Eddie Phillipson, with the last three umpiring in Test matches.

V

VICTORIES

Lancashire's greatest number of victories in a County Championship season is 19 from 32 matches in 1925, when rather surprisingly, the county finished third in the table. Their biggest victory came in 1911 when they beat Hampshire by an innings and 455 runs in the match at Old Trafford, after they had declared their innings at 676 for seven.

W

WARD, ALBERT

Yorkshire-born Albert Ward played for his native county, but without any success and though Lord Hawke asked him to play again in 1888, he declined. A schoolmaster by profession he had taken a teaching job in Leyland and this brought him into contact with the Lancashire Committee. Within twelve months, he had made his Lancashire debut against the MCC at Lord's and a few days later scored 114 not out against Middlesex also at Lord's.

Ward was the first Lancashire professional to score over 1,000 runs in a season's county matches, a feat he achieved on nine occasions. His best season was 1900 when he scored 1,511 runs at 37.77. He scored 24 centuries for the county with a best of 185 against Kent at Gravesend.

He played in 7 Tests for England and scored 117 at Sydney in the first Test of the 1894-95 series. Also on that tour he scored 219 against South Australia at Adelaide to finish as the leading scorer with 916 runs at an average of 41, yet he never represented his country again. Playing the last of his 330 matches in 1904, he scored 15,392 runs at 30.96.

WARD, ALBERT.
LANCASHIRE.

WARTIME

First World War

Throughout the hostilities, Lancashire's members remained faithful and around 1,700 of them continued to pay their subscriptions for the duration of the war. Their money enabled the county to survive and also eased the wartime problems with donations and kit for prisoners of war. Yet at the same time, it fulfilled their obligations to the players on the staff who were dispersed to various war duties from which some of them were never to return. Harold Garnett, Alfred Hartley, W.K. Tyldesley, T.A. Nelson and Egerton L. Wright were all killed.

The Old Trafford Pavilion became a hospital – it was called the Pavilion Hospital – and remained so until February 1919, when they unveiled a tablet honouring Lancashire's dead.

Second World War

When war was declared, the Old Trafford ground, buildings and all, was requisitioned by the Army and the Royal Engineers moved in. One of the earliest casualties was former Lancashire captain Peter Eckersley, who was killed in a flying accident. Old Trafford was blitzed at the beginning of 1941 with damage to the pavilion and bomb craters on the field of play. The Ministry of Supply took over the ground as a dump for vehicles and equipment necessary to the fighting forces.

The county's leading players, almost all of them in uniform found time for an occasional game in aid of war charities. In 1941 for example, a Lancashire team played West Indies in a 12-a-side one-day match at Fazakerley. Three service matches were played in 1944 and at the end of that season, the Lancashire Committee met to plan for a resumption of first-class cricket.

Several matches were staged in 1945, including two against Yorkshire, one of which was first-class and played at Bradford for the benefit of Hedley Verity's widow and children. A three day 'Victory' Test was played at Old Trafford, with England beating Australia by six wickets.

A £100,000 appeal was launched 'to men of goodwill' to re-build Old Trafford. Unfortunately, this figure was not reached and the fund closed with a total of £42,236, which did not allow for the total rebuilding of the Old Trafford pavilion.

WARWICKSHIRE

Founded in 1882, Warwickshire have won the County Championship five times in 1911, 1951, 1972, 1994 and 1995. The county also won the Gillette Cup in 1966 and 1968, the Nat West Trophy in 1989, 1993 and 1995 and the Benson and Hedges Cup in 1994. They also took the Sunday League in 1980 and 1994.

In 1895, J.T. Tyldesley in only his second match for the county, scored 152 not out in Lancashire's innings win. It was the first of eleven centuries that he was to score at Edgbaston, his favourite ground.

In the match at Blackpool in 1959, Jim Stewart of Warwickshire hit 17 sixes, a record in first-class cricket. He hit 10 in the first innings, one short of the world record and seven in the second as he scored 155 and 125 but still Warwickshire could only manage a draw.

In the 1969 County Championship match at Nuneaton, the same free-scoring Jim Stewart was involved in a remarkable last over finish. The home side needed 5 runs to win from the games' last six deliveries with five wickets standing. Ken Higgs bowled Tom Cartwright and Eddie Hemmings, leaving Stewart to get two runs. He failed to get one and Lancashire got a draw.

Neil Fairbrother's debut innings came in the match against Warwickshire at Edgbaston in 1983. The two captains, Abrahams and Willis had agreed that Lancashire would declare their innings closed at 250 to set up a victory chase. Fairbrother was six short of his hundred when 250 was reached. Willis could have given the Lancashire batsman the necessary deliveries to reach three figures, but he turned on his heels and headed back to the pavilion, much to the disgust of several players.

Lancashire's record of first-class matches v Warwickshire is:

P.	W.	L.	D.	Tied
173	59	31	83	0

WASHBROOK, CYRIL

Considered something of a cricketing prodigy, Cyril Washbrook was offered games with the Minor County sides of both Lancashire and Warwickshire. His father was hoping he would go to Birmingham University, and so join Warwickshire, but he didn't and on leaving school he joined Lancashire as a professional. His first Minor Counties game as a member of the Lancashire ground staff was against Yorkshire at Bradford in 1933, where he hit a double century.

His first appearance for the full county side was against Sussex at Old Trafford in that summer of 1933 and after opening the batting in the second innings, he scored 40. In the next match against Surrey, also at Old Trafford, he scored 152, the first of 58 centuries for Lancashire.

In 1937, he made his international debut, playing for England against New Zealand at the Oval. He went on to represent his country on 37 occasions, scoring 2,569 runs at an average of 42.81 and a highest score of 195 against South Africa in Johannesborg in the 1948-49 series.

When cricket resumed in 1946, Washbrook scored 1,938 runs for the county at 71.77, one of sixteen occasions that he scored over 1,000 runs in a season. Runs continued to flow from his bat and fine qualities as an opening batsman, both with Hutton for England and Place for Lancashire shone through.

He was appointed Lancashire's captain in 1954, a position he held until 1959 when he played the last of his 500 matches for the county. He had scored 27,863 runs at an average of 42.15. Appointed on to the Lancashire Committee, he became the county side's manager in 1968 and in 1988 was elected President of the County Club.

Cyril Washbrook

WASIM AKRAM

Arguably the world's best all-rounder, Wasim Akram made his impact felt early on in 1988, his first season with the county. Playing against Surrey at Southport, the Pakistani performed the hat-trick and then hit 98 off 78 deliveries. In 1989, he topped the Lancashire bowling averages with 50 wickets at 19.86 runs apiece but the following summer suffered groin problems and only played in six of the county's Championship matches.

In 1991, he was bowling at his fastest and looked to be on the way to taking 100 wickets. Unfortunately, a foot injury prevented him from finishing the season and he had to be content with topping the county's bowling averages again with 56 wickets at 22.33 runs each.

The following summer he was missing from the Lancashire side, touring England with Pakistan, he topped his country's bowling averages in the five Tests with 21 wickets at 22.00 runs each and a best of six for 67 at the Oval.

Wasim Akram

In 1993, he was only available until mid-season, but again headed the bowling averages with 59 wickets at 19.27 runs apiece, including career best figures of eight for 68 against Yorkshire. The following season he improved on these figures when taking eight for 30 against Somerset at Southport. In 1995, he had his best season to date for Lancashire, taking 81 wickets at 19.72 runs each and took ten wickets in a match on three occasions.

Currently the Pakistan captain, he hit a career best 257 against Zimbabwe in October 1996 and in the process broke two records. He hit the most sixes in a Test and established a new eighth wicket stand of 313 with Saqlain Mushtaq.

Appointed Lancashire's vice-captain for the 1997 season, he will the following year follow in the footsteps of Farokh Engineer and Clive Lloyd in becoming the county's third overseas player to be awarded a benefit.

WATKINSON, MIKE

Lancashire's captain earned his county cap the hard way, for after making his debut in 1982, he had made 195 first team appearances by the end of 1987, the summer in which he was capped. A marvellous one-day player, he has often been the difference between winning and losing, both with the bat and the ball and with both seam and spin.

In 1992, he performed the hat-trick against Warwickshire at Edgbaston and the following year, scored 1,016 runs and took 51 wickets, the first time for thirty years that anyone had achieved this feat for the county. In 1994, Watkinson became only the third player in the county's history to score a century and take ten wickets in a match, a feat he achieved in the match against Hampshire at Old Trafford. It was in this match that he produced his best ever bowling figures when he took eight for 30. His best score with the bat for Lancashire came the following season when he made 161 against Essex at Old Trafford.

In 1995, he made his England debut against the West Indies on his home ground and scored 37 and took five wickets in the match for 92 runs. At Trent Bridge, he scored a superb unbeaten 82 to save England from defeat.

Mike Watkinson

He was appointed county captain in 1994 and though he has led the county to success in both the Benson and Hedges Cup and Nat West Trophy, all Lancashire supporters are hoping that 'Winker' can bring the County Championship title to Old Trafford outright for the first time in sixty-three years.

WATSON, ALEC

Born in Coatbridge in Scotland, Alec Watson played his first game for the county in 1871 and in his early days bowled well in harness with Bill McIntyre. The two became the scourge of Surrey and bowled unchanged in both matches of 1873, helping to dismiss the home side for just 33 in the match at the Oval.

Thought to be one of the best slow bowlers in the country, he represented the Players against the Gentlemen in 1877 and in 1886 took six for 8 in 15 overs as Lancashire beat the MCC inside a day at Lord's. The following season, he took 100 wickets at a cost of 14.82

runs apiece and in 1889 at the age of 45, finished fourth in the national averages with 90 wickets at 12.65 runs each.

Playing his last game for the county in 1893, he took 1,308 wickets at a cost of only 13.39 runs apiece, making him one of the most successful bowlers in the county's history.

WATSON, FRANK

During his first-class career, the solid and dependable Frank Watson scored 49 centuries for Lancashire, including three double centuries and a treble century, when he scored 300 not out against Surrey at Old Trafford in 1928. That summer he scored 2,541 runs for the county at an average of 65.74, his wicket being one of the most difficult in England to take.

He never achieved selection for the full England side though he did tour the Caribbean with an MCC side in 1925-26 and scored a century against Jamaica at Kingston, batting at Number 10. Unfortunately, Watson's career was brought to a premature end by a rising ball from Yorkshire's Bill Bowes. There were fears that the Lancashire batsman would lose an eye, but happily they proved to be groundless.

Though never regarded as a bowler, he took 402 wickets at 31.86 runs each to go with the 22,833 runs he scored for the county at an average of 37.06.

WEATHER CONDITIONS

Many Lancashire matches have been curtailed due to rain and bad light but in June 1975 after Lancashire had scored 477 for five on a beautiful sunny Saturday, it snowed the following Monday.

Derbyshire who had lost two wickets on the Saturday evening, were bowled out for 42 and 87 on the Tuesday to lose by an innings and 348 runs. Conversely, in July 1868, a game between Surrey and Lancashire at the Oval was suspended for one hour because of the intense heat.

WEST INDIES

The first West Indian touring party to England set sail aboard RMS

Trent leaving Barbados on 26 May 1900 and arriving in Southampton a record-breaking ten days later. Their first visit to Old Trafford that summer saw them well beaten, but Aucker Warner, 'Plum' Warner's brother who captained the side, was hampered by the fact that, instead of picking the strongest party, he was obliged to take a representative selection from all the islands.

In 1941, the West Indies played Lancashire in a 12-a-side one-day match at Fazakerley. It was 1950 before a team from the Caribbean defeated Lancashire and as they beat the Red-Rose county by an innings and 220 runs on an adjacent wicket to the one to be used for the first Test at Old Trafford, they derived much encouragement. Scoring 454 for seven, their highest score in these matches, the West Indies bowled out Lancashire for 103 and 131 with Alf Valentine having match figures of thirteen for 67, including eight for 26 in Lancashire's first innings. Lancashire's record of first-class matches v West Indies is:

P.	W.	L.	D.	Tied
15	1	4	10	0

WHALLEY

The ground's one and only first-class match was played on 20, 21 and 22 June 1867. It was the first official Lancashire v Yorkshire match, Yorkshire winning by an innings and 56 runs.

Whalley have never since staged a first-class match. However, they did provide Lancashire with its most successful captain, Leonard Green, who captained Lancashire from 1926 to 1928 when they won the County Championship in all three seasons. Whalley remains one of the county's most pleasant grounds and the Club play in the Ribblesdale Cricket League.

WHARTON, ALAN

An attacking left-handed batsman and more than useful right-arm medium-pace bowler, Alan Wharton made his debut for Lancashire in 1946. His batting was instinctive in his first season, he hit hundreds against Leicestershire and Northamptonshire. In 1949, he scored four centuries and became one of only nine Lancashire League amateurs to graduate to international cricket. He made his Test debut for England against New Zealand at Headingley. Injury forced him to miss the next Test and he never played for England again.

Wharton's bowling which brought him 225 wickets for the county was never to be underestimated and in 1951, he took seven for 33 against Sussex at Old Trafford. Unbelievably, after scoring 2,157 runs at an average of 40.69 in 1959, included his highest score of 199 against Sussex at Hove, he was asked to captain the second team!

At the end of the 1960 season, he ended his career with Lancashire in which he had scored 17,921 runs at 33.55 and joined Leicestershire. At Grace Road he scored centuries in each innings of a match with Middlesex and with Willie Watson set a new county third-wicket partnership of 316 against Somerset at Taunton in 1961.

Elected vice-president of the Lancashire County Cricket Club in 1990, he was appointed President of the Lancashire Former Players' Association in the summer of 1993, shortly before his death.

WICKET-KEEPERS

The following wicket-keepers have made the most dismissals for Lancashire.

	Played	Matches	Caught	Stumped	Total
G. Duckworth	1923-38	424	634	288	922
W.K. Hegg	1987-96	200	480	61	541
R. Pilling	1877-89	177	333	153	486
F. Engineer	1968-76	175	429	35	464
C. Smith	1893-1902	167	312	119	431
G. Clayton	1959-64	183	390	32	422
A. Wilson	1948-62	171	287	59	346
W. Farrimond	1924-45	134	232	65	297
W. Worsley	1903-13	136	239	45	284
K. Goodwin	1960-74	122	227	26	253

Warren Hegg and Bill Farrimond hold the county record for the most dismissals in an innings with seven, whilst current Lancashire wicket-keeper Hegg also holds the record for the most dismissals in a match with eleven against Derbyshire at Chesterfield in 1989.

George Duckworth holds the record for the most dismissals in a season with 97 (69 caught and 28 stumped) for Lancashire in 1928.

When the 1930 MCC party to tour South Africa was named, there were as usual two wicket-keepers, but they made strange reading to many as they were Lancashire's George Duckworth and Bill Farrimond.

The mutterings could be heard from down south. How can you have two wicket-keepers from the same county? Bill Farrimond was a brilliant wicket-keeper who first appeared for Lancashire in 1924 during a Test match where George Duckworth was keeping. Thereafter, he was a stand-in for Duckworth, playing two Tests in South Africa for Percy Chapman's team and one in 1935 at Lord's when Les Ames was solely in the side for his batting. In 1938 at the age of 35, he took over behind the stumps for Lancashire when Duckworth retired and kept for two seasons. There were many occasions when other counties approached him with offers, but Farrimond would not leave his beloved Lancashire.

WILKINSON, LEN

After starting his career as a fast bowler with Heaton in the Bolton League, he turned to leg-spin and joined the Lancashire ground staff in 1936. He made his debut the following season against New Zealand and in his first over, dismissed the Kiwi's captain Milford Page.

He had a superb season in 1938, though after eight matches up until the end of May, he had only taken sixteen wickets. Then his fortunes began to change and by the time Lancashire played Kent at Canterbury in early August, he had taken 87 wickets. In this match he produced match figures of twelve for 125 and finished the summer with 145 wickets, a figure that has since only been exceeded by Malcolm Hilton and Roy Tattersall. He toured South Africa with MCC in 1938-39 and played in three Tests.

When cricket resumed after the Second World War, Wilkinson was injured in his first match and had to have a cartilage operation. He played in two Championship matches in 1947, but his county career in which he had taken 232 wickets at 26.25 was at a close.

WOOD, BARRY

Barry Wood played five times for Yorkshire in 1964 before moving to Lancashire two years later. In his first full season for the county, 1967, he scored 1,007 runs at an average of 24.56, a feat he was to repeat on six occasions during his fourteen years with the county.

He formed a formidable opening partnership with David Lloyd and shared in three stands of over 250. It was this kind of form that led to him being selected for England and in 1972 he made the first of 12 appearances for his country against Australia at the Oval, scoring 90 in the second innings.

His all-round ability, both with the bat and ball and in the field was invaluable in the county's reign as an outstanding limited-overs side. Not only did he score 4,331 runs and take 219 wickets in his 203 limited-overs appearances, but he also created a record by being named Man-of-the-Match sixteen times. Controversy seemed to follow Wood around and in 1979 after receiving a benefit cheque for £64,429, he told the Lancashire Committee he wanted more money to re-sign for the 1980 season.

Lancashire announced that he was dissatisfied with the terms and Wood left to play for Derbyshire. He had played in 260 matches, scoring 12,969 runs at an average of 35.24 and captured 251 wickets at a cost of 27.52 runs each. He captained Derbyshire to success in the first ever Nat West Trophy Final at Lord's in 1981 before later leading Cheshire to success over Northamptonshire in the 1988 competition.

WORCESTERSHIRE

Founded in 1865, Worcestershire waited 99 years for their first title, winning the County Championship in 1964. They then promptly won the title again in their Centenary year and again in 1974 before winning it in two successive years, 1988 and 1989. The county have won the Sunday League on three occasions, 1971, 1987 and 1988 and have won the Benson and Hedges Cup in 1991 and the Nat West Trophy in 1994.

When Lancashire met Worcestershire at Old Trafford in 1900, Johnny Briggs took all ten wickets for 55 runs, whilst in 1902, J.T. Tyldesley scored 248 at Aigburth after being dropped first ball!

Barry Wood

Lancashire pulled off a remarkable victory against Worcestershire at Old Trafford in 1912 when they bowled them out twice in under two and three-quarter hours. Lancashire declared their first innings closed at 269 for eight and then bowled Worcestershire out for 47 in 90 minutes. Following-on, the visitors were bowled out for 41 in 70 minutes to give Lancashire victory by an innings and 181 runs, with Harry Dean having match figures of thirteen for 49.

Worcestershire were also Lancashire's opponents when Bob Berry took all ten wickets at Blackpool in 1953. After gaining a first innings lead of 74, Lancashire declared their second innings at 262 for eight. Worcestershire seemed to be struggling at 153 for five with all the wickets having fallen to Berry before Broadbent and Devereux added 104 in 85 minutes. Berry then separated them and took the last four wickets to give Lancashire victory by 18 runs after seven minutes of the extra half-hour. Lancashire's record of first-class matches v Worcestershire is:

P.	W.	L.	D.	Tied
143	55	29	59	0

YORKSHIRE

Founded in 1863, Yorkshire won two unofficial county titles in 1867 and 1870 before going on to take the record number of 29 official Championships, including a sequence of four successive titles between 1922 and 1925. But the once-proud county has not tasted Championship victory since 1968 when, the county having won six of the last nine Championships were led by Brian Close. The strong side of the 1960s won the Gillette Cup in 1966 and 1969 but until 1987 when they won the Benson and Hedges Cup, the only title came in 1983 when they won the Sunday League. The first official Roses match was at the beautiful Whalley ground in 1867, where Lancashire lost by an innings and 56 runs.

After five successive wins for the White-Rose county, Lancashire gained their first victory at Sheffield in 1871. Arthur Appleby batting at Number 8 scored 99 and had match figures of eight for 141. The

Yorkshire player Joe Rowbotham even refused to bowl as Lancashire's total passed 300.

In 1875, Lancashire were set 146 for victory, which in those days was a fairly demanding total. Hornby and Barlow knocked off the runs, Hornby scoring 78 not out and Barlow 50 not out. Hornby received a new cane-handled bat from Lancashire secretary Sam Swire and Barlow was presented with six sovereigns.

The following year, Lancashire looked comfortably placed at 62 for three towards the 89 they needed for victory. The last six wickets fell for 8 runs with Yorkshire's Allen Hill taking five for 1 in four overs.

In 1889, Yorkshire needed only 75 for victory, but Arthur Mold bowled brilliantly so that when Yorkshire's ninth wicket fell, they were still four runs short of their target. Last man Willie Middlebrook skyed the ball to Hornby who safely held it to give Lancashire victory by 3 runs.

Between 1889 and 1893, Lancashire had their best period in the history of Roses cricket, winning eight and losing only one of the ten matches played. Arthur Mold was still terrorising the Yorkshire batsmen and on a rain-affected Huddersfield wicket, took nine for 41 as Lancashire won by an innings and 28 runs. His last eight wickets came in 8.1 overs for 13 runs.

At Old Trafford in 1893, Yorkshire required 57 to win but by lunch on the final day, had slipped to 42 for six. Yorkshire's last pair of Ulyett and Hunter took the score to 51 and with six needed for victory, Johnny Briggs waved Albert Ward to the boundary rails directly behind him. Briggs then fed Ulyett a tempting ball which he hit high towards Ward, who held a brilliant catch.

In 1911, Kenneth MacLeod scored one of the fastest centuries in Roses matches. His hundred took 110 minutes and he went on to score 121 in 125 minutes with three 6's and fifteen 4's. An extra Roses match was arranged for 1913 to coincide with the visit to Liverpool of King George V and Queen Mary. Harry Dean turned in the out-standing bowling performance in Lancashire's history with nine for 62 and eight for 29 to give him match figures of seventeen for 91 as Lancashire won a low scoring match by three wickets.

At Old Trafford in 1922, Yorkshire ended the first day on 108 for six after bowling Lancashire out for 118. There was no play on the second day but Yorkshire bowled out for 122, then dismissed Lancashire a second time for 135. Needing 132 to win, they reached the final over with their last pairing of Wilfred Rhodes and Rockley Wilson at the wicket and five runs still required. Rhodes blocked the first four deliveries of Parkin's over and the fifth was a no ball, but still the Yorkshire great refused the chance of a winning hit and took a single off the last ball.

In 1924 in the match at Headingley, Yorkshire were bowled out for 33 when needing 58 to win. In a low scoring match, Dick Tyldesley took six for 18 (ten for 87 in the match) and Cec Parkin three for 15 (eight for 61).

The 1960 meeting at Old Trafford saw Lancashire require just 78 to win in two hours. At one stage, the Red-Rose county were 43 for six but even though Grieves and Clayton rescued the situation, they reached the last ball still needing 3 to win. Jack Dyson edged it off his toes for four – Lancashire had won by two wickets and completed their first double over their rivals since 1893.

Lancashire's record of first-class matches v Yorkshire is:

P.	W.	L.	D.	Tied
240	48	76	116	0

YOUNG CRICKETER OF THE YEAR

The annual award made by The Cricket Writers' Club (founded in 1946) is currently restricted to players qualified for England and under the age of 23 on 1 April. Five Lancashire players have been selected and they are as follows:

1950	Roy Tattersall
1959	Geoff Pullar
1975	Andrew Kennedy
1990	Michael Atherton
1994	John Crawley

YOUNGEST

The youngest cricketer to appear for Lancashire is Peter Marner who was 16 years 150 days old when he made his debut in the County Championship match against Sussex at Hove in 1952.

Z

ZENITH

The most glorious period in Lancashire's occurred when Leonard Green captained the county for three years, 1926 – 1928 and they won the Championship in each of them. After the hat-trick of Championships, they won the title again in 1930, after being runners-up in 1929 and then for the eighth time in their history, were champions in 1934.

ZIMBABWE

Lancashire and Zimbabwe, the latest country to be admitted to Test match status have met on two occasions, with the Red-Rose county still waiting to taste victory. Lancashire toured Zimbabwe prior to the start of the 1989 season and were beaten by ten wickets in the match at the Harare Sports Club.

At Old Trafford in May 1990, Nick Speak scored a maiden first-class century as he and Graham Lloyd put on 154 in a fluent opening partnership, but Zimbabwe never attempted their target of 260 in 40 overs and the game ended in a draw. Lancashire's record of first-class matches v Zimbabwe is:

P.	W.	L.	D.	Tied
2	0	1	1	0

Index

A

Abrahams, John, 1, 12, 23, 79
Aigburth, 2
Akram, Wasim, 95, 117, 121
Allen, Gubby, 68
Allott, Paul, 3, 117, 121
Ames, Les, 137
appearances, 4
Appleby, Arthur, 5, 140
Aston Villa, 45, 107
Atherton, Michael, 5, 36, 41, 60, 87, 104, 121, 142
attendances, 7
Australia, 4 - 5, 7, 10, 13, 18 - 19, 28, 33, 35, 44 - 45, 55, 67 - 68, 74, 77, 80 - 81, 85, 93, 97, 99 - 100, 103, 106, 108, 113, 114, 122, 125, 138

B

Bailey, Trevor, 122
bails, 8
bat, carrying, 24
Baker, George, 11
Barber, Bob, 9, 23, 92, 121
Bardswell, Gerald, 9
Barlow, Alf, 122
Barlow, Richard, 10, 24, 45, 56, 121
Barnes, Sydney, 10, 86, 121
Bates, Willie, 26
Bedi, Bishen, 66, 90
benefits, 11
Benson and Hedges Cup, 12
Berry, Bob, 4, 13, 90, 121, 140
Birmingham City, 46
Blackburn Rovers, 45, 64
Blackledge, Joe, 9, 14, 23
Blackpool, 109
Boddington, 56
Bolton Wanderers, 45, 116
Bond, Jack, 15, 23, 49, 65, 77, 126
books, 17
Booth, Brian, 24

Bowes, Bill, 134
Bowes, John, 126
Boycott, Geoff, 108
Bradman, Don, 8, 60
Brearley, Walter, 18, 57, 86, 111, 121
Briggs, Johnny, 4, 11, 19, 33, 35, 66, 86, 100, 104, 118 - 119, 121, 138, 141
brothers, 21
Brown, Freddie, 13, 114
Bull, Fred, 40
Burnley, 45, 87, 116
Bury, 46
Buse, Bertie, 94, 111
Butler, Alexander, 21
Butterworth, H., 104

C

Cambridge University, 2, 5, 9, 12, 22, 30, 53, 104, 114
Cartwright, Tom, 129
Castleton, 24, 56
catches, 25
centuries, 25
championships, 26 - 27
Chapman, Percy, 70, 137
Chappell, Ian, 95
Chapple, Glen, 40
Cheshire, 3, 31, 138
Chorley, 14
Christmas Card, 28
Clayton, Geoff, 89, 136
clergymen, 28
Close, Brian, 140
Combined Universities, 5, 12, 38
Cook, Lol, 29, 34, 56, 91
Cranston, Ken, 23, 29, 33, 121
Crawley, John, 13, 30, 80, 121, 142
Croft, Colin, 13, 95, 121
Croome, Arthur, 51
Crosfield, Sydney, 23, 31, 64
Cumberland, 38, 79, 87
Cumbes, Jim, 46
Cuttell, Willis, 11, 25, 31, 35, 121

D

de Freitas, P., 87, 121
de Silva, Aravinda, 70
Dean, Harry, 2, 32, 56, 70, 86, 121,
    140 - 141
Denton St Lawrence, 13
Derby County, 116
Derbyshire, 13, 29, 32, 40, 45 - 46, 58,
    60, 65, 79, 81, 87, 93, 124 - 125, 134,
    136, 138
Dipper, Alf, 51
double centuries, 35
Douglas, Johnny, 40, 97
Duckworth, George, 11, 35, 42, 70, 92,
    121, 136
Durham, 7, 36, 47, 111
Durham University, 46
Dyson, Jack, 46, 95, 142

E

East Lancashire, 36
Eastman, George, 40
Eckersley, Peter, 23, 27, 37, 74, 100,
    128
Edrich, Bill, 84
Edrich, Geoff, 22, 38
Elliott, Harry, 126
Enfield, 5
Engineer, Farokh, 38 - 39, 95, 121, 132,
    136
Essex, 5, 14, 30, 40, 44 - 45, 60, 87,
    108, 117, 122, 132
Evans, Godfrey, 52
Everton, 45, 83, 107

F

Fairbrother, Neil, 12, 23, 41, 60, 104,
    121, 122, 129
Fallows, Jack, 23, 42
Farnworth, 65
Farrimond, Bill, 42, 70, 121, 136
Fender, Percy, 73
Fenley, Stan, 119
Flack, Bert, 54
footballers, 45
Fowke, Major, 72
Fowler, Graeme, 3, 13, 25, 43, 46 - 47,
    87, 89, 106, 112, 117. 121

G

Gallian, Jason, 13, 34, 60, 93, 121
Garnett, Harold, 128
Gatting, Mike, 3
Gilbert, Walter, 50
Gillette Cup, 48 - 49
Glamorgan, 14, 24, 31, 36, 39, 58, 79,
    98, 101, 103, 110
Gloucestershire, 17, 32, 37, 48, 63, 65,
    77, 87, 94, 103 - 104, 116 - 117, 124
Goodwin, Fred, 45
Goodwin, K., 136
Gower, David, 3, 7
Grace, E.M., 50
Grace, G.F., 50
Grace, W.G., 5, 50, 60, 85, 114, 122
Grappenhall, 41
Green, David, 123
Green, Leonard, 23, 27, 37, 52, 91, 135,
    143
Greenhough, Tommy, 52, 121
Greenidge, Gordon, 2
Greenwood, Peter, 46
Gregson, Bill, 14, 72
Grieves, Ken, 4, 23, 25, 46, 53, 69, 85,
    95
groundsmen, 54

H

Hallam, Maurice, 73
Hallows, Charlie, 24, 26, 55, 85, 88, 90,
    93, 121, 122
Hallows, J., 35
Hammond, Wally, 2, 51, 122
Hampshire, 4, 13, 15, 25, 38, 52,
    56 - 60, 64, 92, 99, 116 - 117, 122,
    127, 132
Hardcastle, Frank, 100
Harris, Lord, 5, 9, 24, 69
Hartley, Alfred, 128
Haslingden, 74, 95
hat-tricks, 56
Hawke, Lord, 11, 106, 127
Hayes, Frank, 23, 57, 69, 110, 121
Hayhurst, Andy, 117
Hayward, Tom, 118
Heap, Jim, 90
Hegg, W.K., 136
Henriksen, Soren, 95

Hickton, Bill, 4, 56, 58
Higgs, Ken, 46, 58 - 59, 71, 86, 121, 129
Hill, Allen, 105, 141
Hilton, Malcolm, 60 - 61, 121, 137
Hobbs, Jack, 11, 119
Hodgson, Gordon, 45
Holding, Michael, 95
Hopwood, Len, 24, 35, 63, 121
Hornby, A.H., 23, 25, 43, 63, 104, 111
Hornby, A.N., 23 - 24, 26, 31, 43, 45,
    51, 56, 63, 64, 89, 92, 106, 110,
    121 - 122
Howard, Nigel, 23, 65, 121, 123
Huddleston, William, 8
Hughes, David, 4, 12, 23, 48, 51, 65,
    90, 117
Humpage, Geoff, 112
hundred, fastest, 43
Hyderabad, 38

I

I'Anson, John, 54
Iddison, Roger, 25, 67, 118
Iddon, Jack, 4, 25 - 26, 67, 85, 104, 121
Ikin, Jack, 24, 42, 68, 121
Illingworth, Ray, 59, 108
India, 4, 38, 41, 47, 52 - 53, 65, 68, 77,
    103, 112
Ingleby-Mackenzie, Colin, 56
injuries, 69
innings, highest, 60
Iqbal, Asif, 49

J

Jefferies, Steve, 95
Jones, Ernest, 89

K

Kallicharran, Alvin, 112
Keighley, 98
Kemble, Arthur, 119
Kemp, Sir George, 100
Kennedy, Alex, 50, 56, 104
Kennedy, Andrew, 142
Kent, 12, 15, 17, 24, 32 - 33, 41 - 42,
    44, 47 - 49, 56, 58, 60, 69, 77, 80 - 81,
    85, 98, 104, 114, 125, 127, 137
Kenyon, Myles, 23, 70
Kermode, A., 104

L

Lancaster, 71
Lara, Brian, 111
Lawson, Geoff, 95
Lee, Peter, 67, 71
Leeds United, 45
Leek Highfield, 11
Leese, Sir Joseph, 100
Leicestershire, 12, 14, 26, 38, 43,
    47 - 50, 59, 63, 72, 74, 77, 83, 88, 92,
    94, 96, 104, 107, 117, 135
Lever, Peter, 73, 89, 121
Leyland Motors, 67
Lindwall, Ray, 8
Lister, Lionel, 23, 74, 91
Liverpool, 45
Liverpool CC, 2
Lloyd, Clive, 2, 12, 49, 74 - 75, 79, 84,
    95, 117, 121, 132
Lloyd, David, 23, 26, 43, 50, 77, 89,
    121, 126, 138
Lloyd, Graham, 44, 80, 113, 143
Londesborough, Lord, 19
Longsight, 13
Lorimer, Rev Malcom, 86
Lyon, J., 104
Lytham, 79

M

McDonald, Ted, 56, 70, 83, 86 - 87, 95,
    123
McFarlane, Les, 112
McIntyre, Bill, 24, 81, 133
MacLaren, Archie, 9, 23, 25, 27, 31, 33,
    60, 64, 80, 86, 92, 104, 111, 119, 121,
    125
MacLeod, Kenneth, 95, 141
Makepeace, Harry, 4, 24, 26, 45, 70,
    82, 85, 89, 91, 120
Malone, Mick, 95
Manchester City, 46
Manchester United, 45
Manchester University, 65
Marchant, Frank, 70
Marner, Peter, 48, 72, 83, 111, 142
Marron, Peter, 55, 121
Martin, P., 36, 121
Matthews, Chris, 95
Matthews, Tom, 54

May, Peter, 2, 12
Mendis, Gehan, 3, 24
Middlebrook, Willie, 141
Middlesex, 5, 9, 15, 28, 43 - 45, 48, 50, 57, 74, 79, 84, 87, 93, 105, 113, 127, 136
Midwinter, Bill, 50
Milnrow, 1
Minor Counties, 11 - 12
Mold, Arthur, 8, 11, 40, 57, 70, 84, 86, 89, 121, 123, 141
Morrison, Danny, 95
Mortimore, John, 51
museum, 86
Mushtaq, Saqlain, 132
musical talents, 86

N

Napier, Revd John, 22, 28
Nash, George, 111
Nash, Malcom, 58, 110
Nat West Trophy, 87
Nelson, 31, 80, 87
Nelson, T.A., 128
Neston, 30, 67
New South Wales, 53
New Year's Card, 88
New Zealand, 47, 68, 82, 88, 95, 103, 114, 130, 136 - 137
Newton-le-Willows, 65
nicknames, 89
no-balls, 89
Northamptonshire, 3, 12, 15, 37, 44, 59, 62, 71, 79, 87, 90, 93, 110, 126, 135, 138
Northern League, 14
Nottinghamshire, 7, 10, 13, 15, 17, 19, 24 - 26, 28, 32 - 33, 37 - 38, 42, 46, 58, 68, 83, 85, 91, 100, 104 - 105, 120, 125
Nutter, Albert, 90

O

O'Shaughnessy, Steve, 26, 64, 73
Old Trafford, 93
Oldfield, Norman, 89, 92, 109, 121, 126
one-day finishes, 94
openers, 94
overseas players, 95

Oxford University, 9, 12, 53, 60, 64, 68, 95, 100, 105

P

Page, Milford, 137
Pakistan, 31, 47, 96, 131
Parker, Paul, 7
Parkin, Cec, 14, 48, 50, 70, 72, 79, 96, 121, 123, 142
Parr, George, 104
partnerships, record, 104
Patterson, Patrick, 95, 121
Paul, Arthur, 106
Paynter, Eddie, 26, 60, 86, 97, 120, 123, 126
Pepper, Cec, 15
Phillips, James, 85, 89
Phillipson, Eddie, 8, 98, 103, 110, 126
Pilling, Dick, 19, 51, 99, 104, 118, 121, 136
Pilling, Harry, 99, 117
Place, Winston, 24, 60, 100, 121, 126
Poidevin, L., 104
Pollard, Dick, 86, 89, 101, 103, 121
Ponsford, Bill, 60
Port Vale, 46
Porthill, 10
presidents, 101
Preston, 103
Preston North End, 45
Procter, Mike, 51
Pullar, Geoff, 8, 12, 89, 103, 121, 142

R

Radcliffe, 15
Ramadhin, Sonny, 95
Ratcliffe, B., 104
Rawtenstall, 53
Reynolds, Fred, 11, 54, 104
Rhodes, Wilfred, 142
Richards, Viv, 94
Richardson, Tom, 118
Ricketts, Jim, 24 - 25, 33, 105
Robinson, Walter, 95
Rochdale, 1, 96
Rowbotham, Joe, 141
Rowley, Edmund, 21, 23, 64, 105
Royle, Vernon, 28, 51, 105, 121, 122
Rugby League, 106

Rugby Union, 106
runner, 106
runs, most, 85
Ryan, Frank, 56

S

Sanderson, Sir Lancelot, 100
Savage, John, 15
Schultz, Sandford, 121, 122
Scotland, 12 - 13
semi-finals, 107
Sharp, Jack, 4, 14, 23, 26, 45, 51 - 52,
  64, 71 - 72, 85, 91, 104, 107, 121, 125
Shastri, Ravi, 110
Sheffield Wednesday, 45, 116
Shropshire, 2
Shuttleworth, Ken, 108, 121
Silverdale, 11
Simmons, Jack, 5, 109
Simpson, Bobby, 93
Singh, Amar, 69
sixes, 110
Skelding, Alec, 72
Smith, 'Big Jim', 84
Smith, C. Aubery, 31
Smith, Charlie, 11, 136
Snow, John, 59
Sobers, Gary, 58, 95, 110
Somerset, 18, 25, 27, 30, 32, 39, 44, 53,
  60, 63, 68, 77, 81, 83, 85 - 86, 88 - 89,
  94, 110 - 111, 117 - 118, 132, 136
South Africa, 7, 11, 13, 19, 29, 30, 31,
  33, 42, 53, 59, 67, 97, 103, 112, 114,
  123, 130
Southport, 112
Speak, Nick, 143
Spofforth, Fred, 7
Spooner, Reg, 104, 106, 113, 121
Sri Lanka, 113
Staffordshire, 68
Statham, Brian, 4, 12, 21, 50, 56, 59,
  86, 89, 92, 114, 121, 125
Steel, A.G., 22, 114 - 115, 121
Steel, D.Q., 21
Steel, E.E., 21
Steel, H.B., 21
Stephenson, John, 80
Stewart, Jim, 15, 129
Stockport, 53

Stockport County, 46
Stoddart, A.E., 82
Studd, G.B., 22
Studd, J.E.K., 22
Sugg, Frank, 11, 34, 45, 116, 121
Sunday League, 116 - 117
Surrey, 3, 5, 7, 15, 19, 24 - 26, 30, 33,
  41 - 42, 44, 53, 60, 64 - 65, 67, 93 - 94,
  100, 103 - 105, 107, 110, 117 - 118,
  122, 130 - 131, 133 - 134
Sussex, 5, 7, 13, 25, 27, 30, 33, 44, 48,
  53, 58, 60, 72, 80 - 83, 94, 98 - 99,
  103 - 104, 110, 114, 119, 130, 136,
  142
Swire, Sam, 141

T

Tasmania, 110
Tate, Maurice, 98
Tattersall, Roy, 86, 91, 111, 120, 121,
  137, 142
team score, highest, 60
Tennyson, Lionel, 37
test cricketers, 121
thousand runs, 122
tied matches, 122
Titchard, S., 87
Tolchard, Roger, 73
Tranmere Rovers, 46
Transvaal, 57
Trumper, Victor, 18
Tyldesley, Dick, 25, 50 - 51, 53, 57, 70,
  72, 86, 119, 121, 125, 142
Tyldesley, Ernest, 4, 12, 21, 25 - 26, 44,
  71, 77, 85, 87, 90 - 91, 104, 121 - 125
Tyldesley, J.T., 2, 21, 25 - 26, 35, 60,
  71, 85, 91, 104, 111, 118, 121,
  123 - 125, 129, 138
Tyldesley, W.K., 128
Tyson, Frank, 114

U

umpires, 126
undefeated, 126
Underwood, Derek, 15

V

Valentine, Alf, 135

Verity, Hedley, 128
victories, 127

W

Walkden, 15
Walker, R.D., 45
Walker, V.E., 45
Walker, Vyell Edward, 84, 93
Wallasey, 63
Ward, Albert, 24, 34, 119, 121, 127, 141
Warner, 'Plum', 135
wartime, 128
Warwickshire, 2, 7, 9, 11 - 15, 17, 32,
    40 - 41, 44, 47 - 48, 57, 66, 71, 77,
    83; 88, 99, 101, 104, 106, 111 - 112,
    123 - 124, 129 - 130, 132
Washbrook, Cyril, 4, 8, 12, 24, 26, 29,
    85, 92, 100, 103, 121, 122, 130
Wasim Akram, 131
Watkinson, Mike, 23, 57, 121, 132
Watson, Alec, 24, 56, 67, 86, 133
Watson, Frank, 4, 26, 35, 37, 55, 60,
    85, 90, 104, 134
Watson, Willie, 136
weather conditions, 134
Werneth, 60
West Bromwich Albion, 46
West Indians, 14 - 15
West Indies, 2, 4, 9, 33, 38, 42, 55, 58 -
    59, 67 - 68, 77, 93, 99, 123, 128, 132,
    134
Westhoughton, 43
Whalley, 56, 135, 140
Wharton, Alan, 85, 94, 121, 135
Whitehead, Ralph, 25, 33
wicket-keepers, 136
wickets, most, 86
Widdowson, Arthur, 54
Widnes Cricket Club, 19
Wilkinson, Len, 121, 137
Willis, Bob, 4
Wilson, A., 136
Wilson, Rockley, 142
Windward Islands, 53
Wood, Barry, 13, 50, 77, 89, 104, 121,
    138
Worcestershire, 4, 8, 12 - 13, 15, 17,
    21, 36, 44, 49, 55, 66, 74, 82, 87, 107,
    112, 117, 138 - 139

Worsley, Bill, 91, 136
Wright, Egerton L., 128
Wright, Rev Frank, 25, 28, 119

Y

Yates, G., 33
Yorkshire, 7, 9, 11 - 13, 22, 24, 26 - 29,
    32 - 34, 42, 58 - 59, 67 - 68, 84, 94,
    105, 113 - 114, 116, 125, 130, 132,
    135, 138, 140 - 141
Young Cricketer of the Year, 142

Z

Zenith, 143
Zimbabwe, 143